Drawing insight from Script ministry, Bishop John Howe . _____ Spirit in the life of Jesus and in the teaching of St. Paul, and he affirms the reality and full range of gifts of the Spirit available to the believer and the church today.

—THE REV. DR. STEPHEN F. NOLL
VICE CHANCELLOR
UGANDA CHRISTIAN UNIVERSITY, RETIRED

This fascinating and important study contains a much needed exploration of the role and significance of the Holy Spirit beyond the often explored passages of the coming of the Spirit at Pentecost and the gifts of the Spirit in Paul. It shows convincingly quite how central the Spirit was to the life and ministry of Jesus, and by extension, therefore, how central it should be to us too. Whatever your view on the role of the Holy Spirit in the church today, this study will deepen, widen and enrich it—it is essential reading for all those who seek to live out their lives as faithful followers of Christ.

—PAULA GOODER, D.PHIL
CANON THEOLOGIAN
BIRMINGHAM AND GUILDFORD CATHEDRALS
WRITER AND LECTURER IN BIBLICAL STUDIES

Everything you've always wanted to know about the Holy Spirit. John Howe, with great wisdom and a wonderfully readable style has put all the pieces together to invite us into a fresh experience of God's life in us and the world. This is the go-to work for both veterans and beginners. If you need to be convinced— or reminded—that the Holy Spirit is alive and active in society today, this is the book for you.

—THE RIGHT REV. WILLIAM C. FREY
EPISCOPAL BISHOP OF COLORADO, RETIRED

In this study, at once astutely biblical and disarmingly personal, Bishop John Howe demonstrates the centrality of the work of the Holy Spirit in the ministry of Jesus and the earliest Christians as promised in the Old Testament and narrated in the New. We have then here a much needed biblical theology of the ministry of the Holy Spirit not as an autopsy of apostolic texts and times, nor as the narrow fixation of a contemporary subset of Christians—but as the personal, gracious, and powerful work of the Spirit as the normal experience of the Church and her members carrying out the mission of God. This, then, is a living theology inviting Christian readers of all sorts to enjoy and share the goodness of the gifts of the Spirit. May it be so.

—GARWOOD P. ANDERSON
ASSOCIATE PROFESSOR OF NEW TESTAMENT AND GREEK
ASSOCIATE DEAN FOR ACADEMIC AFFAIRS
NASHOTAH HOUSE THEOLOGICAL SEMINARY

A readable, engaging, scripturally comprehensive account of the anointing of the Holy Spirit and its cruciality in the ministry of Jesus and the Church. Filled with pastoral insight, sensitive to the challenge this important teaching makes for the life of individual Christians and for the Church.

—THE REV. DR. CHRISTOPHER R. SEITZ
CANON THEOLOGIAN, EPISCOPAL DIOCESE OF DALLAS
RESEARCH PROFESSOR OF BIBLICAL INTERPRETATION
WYCLIFFE COLLEGE, TORONTO

In this engaging and provocative work, Bishop Howe has truly broken new ground. Written in a clear and accessible style, this book takes the reader on a journey deep into Scripture and into the life and ministry of Jesus Christ. Offering a unique look at exactly when and how Jesus began his earthly ministry, the Bishop proposes a new idea concerning the role of the Holy Spirit in the ministry of Jesus Christ. From this unique foundation, this book goes on to show why the role of the Holy Spirit is so important in our lives and in our world. Although not all readers may agree with every idea in this book, I am certain that all readers will be stirred in thought, and hopefully, led to a new sense of the importance of the Holy Spirit's work in the life of Jesus Christ, as well as our own.

—PAUL J. KIRBAS, D.MIN, PHD
PAUL TILLICH PROFESSOR OF THEOLOGY AND CULTURE
GRADUATE THEOLOGICAL FOUNDATION

Bishop John Howe offers to the church a treasure of insight through his connection of the gifts of the Holy Spirit to Jesus himself. As we see Christ's anointing more clearly, we are better able to understand God's desire to anoint us with the same Spirit that was upon our Savior. Additionally, Bishop Howe draws from decades of pastoral ministry as a priest and bishop to make theology "come alive" in what he has written.

—Dr. Steve Harper
Professor of Spiritual Formation
Asbury Theological Seminary, Orlando, Florida

Vintage John Howe. Those who have heard John over the years will delight in discovering once again the consummate voice of a gifted Bible teacher whose searing clarity, characteristic lucidity, and forceful scholarship always packs a wallop. Few people in my experience have so demonstrated the supernatural gift of teaching as John, and yet—as always—he wears this anointing with humility and grace. Here you will find a balanced approach to the gifts of the Spirit that will challenge both those on the Reformed and Pentecostal ends of the ecclesiastical spectrum. Plus you will be treated to a lifetime of reflection on the key biblical passages dealing with the work of the Spirit as applied to the practicalities of lay and ordained ministry. Of particular interest is his effort to show that Jesus just may himself have spoken in tongues. Whether you are drawn to agree with everything he says or not, you will be prompted to further study and encouraged to greater openness to the Spirit of Jesus Christ who as he says is the "one who makes us alive in Christ."

—The Rev. Peter C. Moore, D.D.
Dean & President Emeritus
Trinity School for Ministry

The Bible is alive and well in your life! Some Bible study groups rightly read the wonderful stories of Jesus of old. But the majesty of the Bible may cause some to forget that the Holy Spirit is active right now. Bishop Howe reminds us of the power of the Spirit today. He gives us a wake-up call to the power of the Spirit in the lives of each of us. He has done us a personal favor!

—The Rev. John Mulvihill, PhD, S.T.D., D.Min.
Judicial Vicar, Chancery of the Roman Catholic
Archbishop of Chicago

Bishop John Howe's *Anointed by the Spirit* is a thoroughly biblical, well-thought out, "easy to read" and "must be read" book. It should be essential reading for all who are exploring the work of the Holy Spirit in the world and the life of the church, and for all who teach and seek to minister in the power of the Holy Spirit.

—BISHOP DAVID PYTCHES
FORMERLY ANGLICAN BISHOP OF CHILE, BOLIVIA AND PERU
AUTHOR OF *COME, HOLY SPIRIT*

Normal Christianity in the New Testament is a life in which God is present, active and expected. It is life in Christ, life in the Spirit. There is, as a result, an excitement that bubbles through both individual and corporate Christian living. Why then is this vitality so often lacking today? Do we really know what the New Testament tells us of the Holy Spirit in our midst and indwelling us? We need a book, written by a superb biblical teacher and pastor with long experience in congregational life in the Spirit, to open to us, in a practical way, the gift of the Spirit and the gifts of the Spirit. Bishop John Howe is such a teacher and pastor who has walked deeply in the life of the Spirit. In *Anointed by the Spirit* he has written an outstanding book on the Spirit which is profoundly biblical, practical, and experiential. Every pastor needs this book and so does every congregation. It is a joy to read. In Christ we are all anointed by the Spirit; it is time we draw deeply upon this anointing. This book will be a great help in doing just that. I recommend it to all most highly.

—THE RIGHT REVEREND JOHN H. RODGERS, JR., THD
BISHOP IN THE ANGLICAN MISSION IN THE AMERICAS

Bishop John Howe has written a book that draws his readers into the work of the Holy Spirit within the church, and in doing so makes them aware that the gift of God's Spirit is given to each and every member of Christ's body to empower a ministry in which each has a particular part to play. This is a book that is as timely as it is important.

—THE REV. DR. PHILIP TURNER, PHD
DEAN, BERKELEY DIVINITY SCHOOL AT YALE, RETIRED

Across the centuries Christian theology has struggled mightily to understand the famous phrase, "He emptied himself taking upon himself the form of a servant." Of what did he empty himself? That question has been examined with great care. But what is the meaning of his baptism? What did he receive at his baptism that he did not already have? Bishop Howe has provided a thorough discussion of this critical topic. Avoiding the classical pitfall of "Adoptionism," we are led into greater depths of meaning as we seek to understand the significance of the act of God in the descent of the Spirit and the meaning of the heavenly voice. I can highly recommend this work for scholars, parish clergy and thoughtful lay people.

—CANON KENNETH E. BAILEY, TH.D
AUTHOR AND LECTURER IN NEW TESTAMENT
THE ECUMENICAL INSTITUTE
JERUSALEM (EMERITUS)

My friend Bishop John Howe demonstrates that the gifts of the Holy Spirit were so essential in the ministry of Jesus, that Jesus himself becomes the chief model of how the gifts operate. To me, his ministry encourages us as his followers to "strive for" the gifts in our own lives. I enjoyed reading Bishop's examples of how spiritual gifts in the lives of contemporary Christians serve as "on ramps" into new dimensions of ministry.

—STEVE STRANG
CO-FOUNDER, CHARISMA MEDIA AND *CHARISMA* MAGAZINE

Bishop John Howe's analysis of the gifts of the spirit is thorough, refreshing, biblically based, and illustrated throughout by inspired examples from our own day. He has done our Church a great service by pointing to the ways in which—like the earliest Christians—we may be able to discern vocations and ministries by the gifts a person offers. As he says, "There are no 'spare parts' in the body of Christ!" Amen!

—THE VERY REV. DR. JANE SHAW
DEAN, GRACE CATHEDRAL, SAN FRANCISCO

ANOINTED
by the Spirit

ANOINTED
by the Spirit

Bishop JOHN W. HOWE

CREATION
HOUSE

ANOINTED BY THE SPIRIT by Bishop John W. Howe
Published by Creation House
A Charisma Media Company
600 Rinehart Road
Lake Mary, Florida 32746
www.charismamedia.com

Unless otherwise noted, all Scripture quotations are from the New Revised Standard Version of the Bible. Copyright © 1989 by the Division of Christian Education of the National Council of the Churches of Christ in the USA. Used by permission.

Scripture quotations marked KJV are from the King James Version of the Bible.

Scripture quotations marked NIV are from the Holy Bible, New International Version of the Bible. Copyright © 1973, 1978, 1984, International Bible Society. Used by permission.

Scripture quotations marked RSV are from the Revised Standard Version of the Bible. Copyright © 1946, 1952, 1971 by the Division of Christian Education of the National Council of the Churches of Christ in the USA. Used by permission.

Content from *Our Anglican Heritage* used by permission of Wipf and Stock Publishers, www.wipfandstock.com.

Design Director: Bill Johnson
Cover design by Nathan Morgan

Library of Congress Cataloging-in-Publication Data: 2011943895
International Standard Book Number: 978-1-61638-830-0
E-book International Standard Book Number: 978-1-61638-831-7

First edition

12 13 14 15 16 — 987654321
Printed in Canada

DEDICATION

THIS BOOK IS dedicated to the clergy and people of the Episcopal Diocese of Central Florida, where I have shared these teachings in so many congregations, and where I have been supported, loved, and prayed for, for nearly a quarter of a century. Special thanks to the members of the Diocesan Board who approved my finishing this book on a sabbatical in the spring of 2011.

*"The Church has never sufficiently confessed the influence
the Holy Spirit exerted upon the work of Christ."*
—ABRAHAM KUYPER[1]

---

1   Abraham Kuyper, *The Work of the Holy Spirit*, trans. H. de Vries (New York: Funk and Wagnalls, 1900), 97.

A shoot shall come out from the stump of Jesse, and a branch shall grow out of his roots. The spirit of the LORD shall rest upon him, the spirit of wisdom and understanding, the spirit of counsel and might, the spirit of knowledge and the fear of the LORD.

—ISAIAH 11:1–2

The spirit of the Lord God is upon me, because the LORD has anointed me; he has sent me to bring good news to the oppressed, to bind up the brokenhearted, to proclaim liberty to the captives, and release to the prisoners.

—ISAIAH 61:1

[Andrew] first found his brother Simon and said to him, "We have found the Messiah" (which is translated Anointed).

—JOHN 1:41

Many in the crowd believed in him and were saying, "When the Messiah comes, will he do more signs than this man has done?"

—JOHN 7:31

That message spread throughout Judea, beginning in Galilee after the baptism that John announced: how God anointed Jesus of Nazareth with the Holy Spirit and with power.

—ACTS 10:37–38

But it is God who establishes us with you in Christ and has anointed us, by putting his seal on us and giving us his Spirit in our hearts as a first installment.

—2 CORINTHIANS 1:21–22

But you have been anointed by the Holy One, and all of you have knowledge.

—1 JOHN 2:20

Author's Note

I have chosen to work (almost) entirely in English rather than with extensive reference to the Greek text so the body of this work will be accessible to the parishioner as well as to the biblical scholar.

CONTENTS

PREFACE

THE ANOINTING OF the Holy Spirit and the gifts the New Testament says he distributes for ministry remain subjects that deeply divide Christians. On the one hand, there are those who teach that the dramatic and clearly "supernatural" gifts that are discussed primarily in the first half of 1 Corinthians 12 were given by God to confirm the teaching of the apostles and that they ceased after the apostolic age ended and the New Testament was completed. On the other hand, there are those who teach that the gifts are normative and that one in particular—the gift of speaking in tongues—is essential to being "baptized" in, by, or with the Holy Spirit.

It is our conviction that both of these positions derive at least in part from focusing too much on that one passage, 1 Corinthians 12:1–11 (and the way speaking in tongues functions in the Book of Acts), and not seeing it alongside of other passages in the New Testament that name and discuss the Spirit's gifts.

In this study, we will begin with a larger picture of the ministry of the Holy Spirit in the life of Jesus and his followers. We will then look in detail at the nine gifts that St. Paul names in that passage, noting that all of them, with the possible exception of tongues and the interpretation of tongues, were abundantly manifested in Jesus's own ministry. It is our conviction that he functioned in ministry as the Anointed One and thus defined and demonstrated these dramatic gifts, thereby encouraging his followers to seek them as well.

We will then compare the other lists and stand-alone mentions of gifts of the Holy Spirit, several of which were also present in Jesus's ministry, though some were not. Many of the other gifts are not so clearly "supernatural," but all are given by the Spirit to equip the church for ministry. We will attempt to determine how these gifts might continue to function in the lives of Jesus's followers today.

THE KEY PASSAGE

Now concerning spiritual gifts, brothers and sisters, I do not want you to be uninformed. You know that when you were pagans, you were enticed and led astray to idols that could not speak. Therefore I want you to understand that no one speaking by the Spirit of God ever says "Let Jesus be cursed!" and no one can say "Jesus is Lord" except by the Holy Spirit.

Now there are varieties of gifts, but the same Spirit; and there are varieties of services, but the same Lord; and there are varieties of activities, but it is the same God who activates all of them in everyone. To each is given the manifestation of the Spirit for the common good. To one is given through the Spirit the utterance of wisdom, and to another the utterance of knowledge according to the same Spirit, to another faith by the same Spirit, to another gifts of healing by the one Spirit, to another the working of miracles, to another prophecy, to another the discernment of spirits, to another various kinds of tongues, to another the interpretation of tongues. All these are activated by one and the same Spirit, who allots to each one individually just as the Spirit chooses.

—1 CORINTHIANS 12:1–11

FOREWORD

THE THEOLOGIAN EDOUARD Schweizer once observed that "long before the Holy Spirit became an article of the creed, he was a living reality in the experience of the primitive church." Indeed, we can go further and say that, throughout the Bible from the second verse of Genesis to the final verses of the last book of the scriptures, the Spirit of God is present as inspirer, guide, teacher and indweller. That means that we cannot talk about God without, in the same breath, talking about the Holy Spirit. Of course, there are sharp differences between the Old and New Testaments. What is implicit and formless in the Old Testament is made explicit and thoroughly formed, in and through, the presence and teaching of Jesus and his followers.

In this powerful and appealing book, Bishop John Howe takes a fresh look at what we mean by the Holy Spirit and for him the only way to do this is by reference to Jesus, the Anointed One. This is not as obvious as some might think. History reveals that theories about the Spirit have abounded through the centuries leading to confusion as well as division. At the Reformation divisions in the Western Church led to the Catholic Church to focus the Spirit's activity in the Church and particularly through its ministry, sacraments and life. Similarly, the Reformation churches limited the Spirit's role to the scriptures and effective preaching. While this is an oversimplification, these two trends remained the norm until the Pentecostal movement of the twentieth century blew apart this seriously flawed sacramental/scriptural divide to introduce the notion of the Spirit as the ever active, personal, dynamic in the life of every believer.

Of course, that does not solve the mystery of the Holy Spirit neither does it suggest that the Pentecostal/charismatic interpretation resolves all the questions. In fact, they should not, because unresolved questions will always remain, as far as interpreting the Spirit of God is concerned. Donald Coggan, one of my distinguished predecessors once wrote: "When the Holy Spirit comes on men and women there is new life but there is disorder too. But give me this every time. If otherwise I have to put up with cold, lifeless orthodoxy." This seems to be an important element in John Howe's examination of the work of the Spirit in the Church. He finds it in the inseparable link between Christ, the anointed one, and his followers.

This is a wonderfully refreshing book. Bishop Howe takes ideas we have taken for granted and returns them to us recharged and with new insights. He laces his teaching with humor and with illustrations from long experience in Christian ministry. The author hammers home his conviction that nowhere in Christian history and experience does one find any basis for the idea that a victorious Christian life is for a few chosen people only. Indeed, there are no super spiritual Christians, only people like you and me who have learned that a powerful Christian life is Christ's gift to us and one he longs for us to possess.

—George L. Carey
103rd Archbishop of Canterbury

CHAPTER 1

THE ANOINTED ONE

"He has anointed me."

—LUKE 4:18

MORE THAN ANY other person in history, Jesus of Nazareth is remembered for the miracles that abounded throughout his ministry. Nearly every one of them had at least two purposes at the same time. The first was (almost always) to meet someone's need as an expression of love and mercy. Jesus was amazingly available, even when it meant putting aside his own personal needs.

The feeding of the five thousand, for instance, occurred just after the beheading of Jesus's cousin and forerunner, John the Baptist. In the midst of his sorrow and grief, Jesus wanted to be alone with his apostles, but Mark tells us, "As he went ashore, he saw a great crowd; and he had compassion for them, because they were like sheep without a shepherd" (Mark 6:34), so he put aside his own needs, spent the rest of the day teaching, and ended up multiplying the loaves and fish to feed the hungry multitude.

On another occasion, Jesus was with a large crowd gathered around him when a leader from one of the synagogues begged him to come heal his daughter who was "at the point of death" (Mark 5:23). Jesus allowed himself to be interrupted and went to raise her from the dead, but en route to her home he was interrupted again by a woman who had suffered hemorrhages for years. She laid hold of his clothing, and

Jesus was "immediately aware that power had gone forth from him" (Mark 5:29). Jesus stopped to minister to her and commend her faith, in effect allowing an interruption in the midst of an interruption!

But the second reason for Jesus's miracles was that they pointed to a conclusion: that Jesus was and is who he claimed to be—the Son of God.[2]

The word *miracle* means "sign," and it is often translated that way. In writing his gospel, the apostle John is explicit in telling us, "Now Jesus did many other signs in the presence of his disciples, which are not written in this book. But these are written *so that* you may come to believe that Jesus is the Messiah, the Son of God, and that through believing you may have life in his name" (John 20:30–31).

Jesus's ministry was marked by "signs and wonders." It is commonly said, "A sign points to something, and a wonder makes you wonder."

Jesus himself said at one point, "If I am not doing the works of my Father then do not believe me. But if I do them, even though you do not believe me, believe the works, so that you may know and understand that the Father is in me and I am in the Father" (John 10:37).

Of course, there have always been skeptics regarding the miracles attributed to Jesus, even among some who consider themselves his followers. But most Christians believe Jesus did the things the New Testament says he did, and that is part of the reason we believe him to be divine.

This raises the question of *how* Jesus did the signs and wonders, the healings and miracles, which characterized his ministry. Most believers would probably respond by saying, "He was the Son of God; what else would you expect?"

Jesus was, indeed, the Son of God, and to put it even more strongly, he was God come among us as a sinless human being. ("'They shall

---

2   Some have argued that this title is rarely used by Jesus himself except in the fourth gospel, but the pivotal question Jesus asked his disciples was, "Who do you say that I am?" When Peter answered, "You are the Messiah, the Son of the Living God," Jesus's response was, "Blessed are you, Simon, son of Jonah! For flesh and blood has not revealed this to you, but my Father in heaven." Matthew is very clear that it was "*from that time on*" that Jesus began to define his Sonship and the kind of Messiah He would be in terms of suffering, death, and resurrection (cf. Matt. 16:13–23).

name him Emmanuel' which means, 'God is with us'" [Matt. 1:23]). But that is not the biblical explanation of his miracles.

For the first thirty years of his life, Jesus performed no miracles whatsoever.

(There are some fantastic tales in some of the so-called "apocryphal" gospels. The Gospel of Thomas, for instance, has him bringing a dead fish back to life at age three and changing a playmate who offended him into a ram. But the Church catholic has never considered such tales authentic or included such "gospels" among its Scriptures.)

Jesus was God come among us, and yet for the first thirty years of his life he changed no water into wine, he healed no sick people, he cast out no evil spirits, and he raised no one from the dead. He didn't even preach a sermon!

It is sometimes said that he taught the elders in the temple when he was twelve, but, in fact, *he* was asking *them* questions. It is clear there was give-and-take. Luke tells us, "All who heard him were amazed at his understanding and his answers" (Luke 2:47). Obviously, his questions provoked them to inquire of him as well. But he was not there to *teach*; he was there to *learn*.

Apart from his supernatural conception (which his own brothers did not believe [John 7:5]), there was nothing "miraculous" about Jesus for the first thirty years of his life. He was a carpenter's apprentice (and one suspects a very good one!), but he was *not* a miracle-worker.

But at the age of thirty, Jesus insisted upon being baptized. His cousin John was initially horrified. "Me, baptize you?" he said, in effect. "It ought to be the other way around." But Jesus insisted this needed to happen "to fulfill all righteousness" (Matt. 3:15). All four gospels record that as he arose from the waters of the Jordan, "the heavens were opened" (Matt. 3:16), they were "torn apart" (Mark 1:10),[3] "the Holy Spirit descended upon him in bodily form like a dove" (Luke 3:22), and "it remained on him" (John 1:32). Thereafter, Jesus never returned to the carpenter's bench.

He began his ministry by claiming for himself the promise of the

---

3   Note the correspondence of the phrase with the plea to the Lord in Isaiah 64:1.

Holy Spirit's anointing as Isaiah had foretold it (Isa. 61:1): "The Spirit of the Lord is upon me, because *he has anointed me* to bring good news to the poor. He has sent me to proclaim release to the captives and recovery of sight to the blind, to let the oppressed go free, to proclaim the year of the Lord's favor" (Luke 4:18–19).

Jesus's own explanation of his wonder-working ministry was that it sprang not from his *divinity* but from his *anointing*; not from his being the *Son of God*—which he was from before the beginning of creation—but from his becoming the *Anointed One* immediately following his baptism. He was *always* the Son of God; he was *not* always the Anointed One.

Three statements in the first chapter of John's gospel put this understanding into sharp relief.

"In the beginning was the Word, and the Word was with God, and the Word was God" (John 1:1). John deliberately opens his gospel with the same phrase that opened the Book of Genesis: "In the beginning..." The beginning of what? The beginning of everything that ever came into existence. Before anything else in the entire universe existed, there was God. And along with God there was God's "Word," his self-expression.

In his very first sentence, John plunges us into (part of) the mystery of the Trinity: how can the Word be *with* God and *be* God at the same time?

Perhaps a homely human analogy can help to illustrate this.

In attempting to communicate (especially in preaching), people express themselves in a variety of ways. They gesture. They seek eye contact. They use facial expressions and body language. They modulate their tone of voice. But above all, they *speak*. They communicate (as best they can) by means of *words*.

All of these efforts to communicate, taken together, might be called their "word," that is, their self-expression.

A question could then be asked: do other people actually know the *person* who is attempting so diligently to communicate, or do they know that person's *word*, his or her self-expression?

Or is that person and his or her "word" one and the same?

Actually, it is entirely possible they are *not* one and the same. The person in question could be trying to deceive people by putting forward a completely false front. A thoroughly evil person would not want others to know his true self. He would attempt to present himself as someone quite respectable (an Episcopal bishop, perhaps).

So it is possible that in knowing someone's *"word,"* his self-expression, others do not know *him* at all.

But surely there is no such duplicity in God. The Book of James calls him "the Father of lights, with whom there is no variation or shadow due to change" (James 1:17). God's Word, his self-expression, is true. To know his Word is to know God himself. God, and God's expression of himself, existing from before the foundation of the world, are two realities—and yet they are one and the same.

It took the Christian church several centuries to work out its understanding of this, and finally no one fully understands it because there is nothing else like it in our experience. But it was the conviction of the apostles and Jesus's first followers that nothing less than this understanding did justice to what they had known of his life, teaching, death, resurrection, and ascension. *He claimed to be God, and he acted like it.*

When they crucified him for blasphemy, they discovered that death could not hold him: "God raised him up, having freed him from death," thereby vindicating his claims (Acts 2:24).

Jesus could not be dismissed as a liar or a lunatic, nor could he be destroyed as a blasphemer, and the earliest Christians were forced to the conclusion that within the one God, in whom they absolutely believed, there was more than one "Person." There were, in fact, Father and Son. And between them was a third "Person," the Holy Spirit.

St. Augustine, Jonathan Edwards, and C. S. Lewis (along with many others) compared the Holy Spirit to the "family spirit" that is so often present when families get together, a reality that is somehow more than the sum of the parts. Within the one God, the reality of the Father loving the Son and the Son loving the Father is in fact a Spirit of love between them so real that he himself is the third "Person" of the Trinity.

"And the Word became flesh and lived among us, and we have seen his glory, the glory as of a father's only son, full of grace and truth" (John 1:14). God had been expressing himself throughout eternity and for all of creation's history. But at a particular moment approximately two thousand years ago, God expressed himself in a way that was radically different from anything that had ever come before. His Word became a human being.

The Infinite took on finitude. The Immortal embraced mortality. The one who was pure Spirit assumed physical flesh and blood. The Son of God became one of us.

St. Paul pondered this mystery in quoting what most biblical scholars think was one of the earliest Christian hymns: "Jesus...though he was in the form of God, did not regard equality with God as something to be exploited, but emptied himself, taking the form of a slave" (Phil. 2:6–7).

Jesus—from all eternity the Word of God, possessing the "form" or "nature" (NIV) of God (Gk. *morphe)*—"emptied" himself and took on the "form" or "nature" of a human being.

Human being is here defined as a "slave" or a "bondservant." In other words, Jesus became the perfect model of what all of us were intended by God to be: servant/slaves of God and of one another.

In looking at Jesus, the eyes of faith will see two things at once: *what God is like* ("Whoever has seen me has seen the Father" [John 14:9]) and what *we are supposed to be* (servants of God and each other).

But in becoming one of us, of what did he "empty" himself? Not his divine *nature* (how could God cease being God?), but some of his divine *prerogatives*. He gave up the exercise of some of his attributes by accepting human limitations.

Jesus accepted the limitation of *confinement in a body*. Before he became a human being he was, in the words of Martin Luther, "everywhere and nowhere,"[4] just as God the Father is. But as a man, if he was in Galilee and wanted to go to Jerusalem, he had to walk (or ride

---

4   Richard Strier, "Martin Luther and the Real Presence in Nature," *Journal of Medieval and Early Modern Studies* 37 (2007): 271–303.

a donkey), just like anyone else. Theologians would say he gave up *omnipresence*—being everywhere at the same time.

He accepted limitations in *knowledge*. People popularly suppose that he "knew everything," but the record is clear that he did not. He asked, "Who touched me?" when the woman with the hemorrhage was healed (Mark 5:30–31). He asked the disciples, "How many loaves do you have?" (Mark 8:5). He asked the father of the epileptic boy, "How long has this been happening to him?" (Mark 9:21). He asked his disciples, "Do you also wish to go away?" (John 6:67). He admitted he did not know the day or the hour of his own return (Matt. 24:36).

It is hard to imagine the Word of God having to learn to speak human words, but it is clear he did. Theologians would say he gave up *omniscience*—knowing everything.

Perhaps most mysteriously, he accepted limitations in *power*. It is tempting to think of Jesus as some kind of superhero who literally could do anything. But, again, the record is clear. The biblical account states bluntly that when he visited his own hometown, "he could do no deed of power there" because of the unbelief of the people (Mark 6:5).

How Jesus's ability to perform miracles is affected by the faith or the unbelief of others is a subject beyond our present purpose (though we will touch upon this subject in chapter 11). But the point is unavoidable: he was *not* able to do some of the things he wanted to do in Nazareth in spite of the fact he was God come among us. Theologians would say he gave up *omnipotence*—the power to do all things.

The eternal Son of God became a man, and in the process he gave up omnipotence, omniscience, and omnipresence. He accepted limitations.

So the question is: How, then, did he do all of the wonderful things he did?

"John [the Baptist] testified, 'I saw the Spirit descending from heaven like a dove, and it remained on him'" (John 1:32).[5] The ministry of Jesus

---

5 It is interesting to note that when Noah sent out a raven, it returned (Gen. 8:6). Then he sent out a dove for the first time, and it, too, returned (v. 9). He sent out a dove a second time, and it returned with a sprig of olive in its beak (v. 11). And then, seven days

Christ is (also) the ministry of the Holy Spirit. The very word *Christ* (which is the Greek translation of the Hebrew word *Messiah*) means the "Anointed One." It is not a proper name; it is a title. He was always the Son of God. He became one of us. Thirty years later, he became what he had never been previously—the Anointed One.

Jesus's ministry of signs, wonders, miracles, and healings is an expression of his *anointing*, not (primarily) his *divinity*. In this, there is great encouragement for his followers, for his final promise before his ascension was: "You will receive power when the Holy Spirit has come upon you; and you shall be my witnesses in Jerusalem, in all Judea and Samaria, and to the ends of the earth" (Acts 1:8).

In the Gospel of Matthew, he said, "All authority in heaven and on earth has been given to me. Go therefore and make disciples of all nations, baptizing them in the name of the Father and of the Son and of the Holy Spirit, and teaching them everything that I have commanded you" (Matt. 28:18–19).

If the authority was given to *him*, why did he command his *disciples* to "go"? Because they were to go *with his authority* and with the enabling of the same Holy Spirit who enabled him.

But note: they were to teach the new disciples "everything [he had] commanded [them]" (Matt. 28:19). Jesus taught his disciples how to heal and how to cast out evil spirits. The Great Commission included the instruction that these mighty signs and wonders in ministry were to be passed on to subsequent generations of believers.

In effect, he said that the key to his ministry would also be the key to theirs. In the following chapters, we will examine the ministry of Jesus as a pattern for those of his followers. This book is not about miracles only, but about all of the gifts and other ministries of the Holy Spirit. We shall return to the subject of miracles in chapter 12.

But first we must examine Jesus's baptism more closely, for it, too, is a key in the relationship of his followers to Jesus. If he is the

---

later, he sent out the dove for the third time, and it *remained* on the "new creation" of a freshly cleansed earth (v. 12). The "dove" of the Holy Spirit, who had "lighted upon" many people throughout Old Testament history, came and went in doing so, but it/he *remained* on Jesus.

"Christ"—the "Anointed One"—what does it mean for his followers to be called "Christians"? They dare to call themselves the "little anointed ones." "Christian" (Gk. *christianios*) is the diminutive form of "Christ." They (we) are the "little Christs."

CHAPTER 2

THE BAPTISM OF JESUS

"It is proper for us to fulfill all righteousness."

—MATTHEW 3:15

WE CALL JESUS's cousin John "the Baptist," and many people assume John invented the ceremony. Actually, it was widely practiced in the ancient world, although it was not always called "baptism." If a person wanted to leave his or her family, tribe, or people and be joined to another by marriage or treaty, it was common to undergo a ceremonial washing, and the symbolism was obvious: the past is being washed away, in preparation for a new and different future.

For at least two hundred years prior to John's ministry, the Jews practiced baptism. The great rabbi Hillel, an older contemporary of both Jesus and John, was once asked, "Which is more important, baptism or circumcision?" He answered, "Baptism."[6]

That is a remarkable answer, in that circumcision was commanded by God as *the* mark of his covenant with Abraham and the Jewish people: "This is my Covenant, which you shall keep, between me and you and your offspring after you: Every male among you shall be

---

6 The Wisconsin Evangelical Lutheran Synod, on its website, says, "Debates on the subject of proselyte baptism are recorded between rabbinic schools of Shammai and Hillel, both contemporaries of Jesus. Whereas the school of Shammai stressed circumcision as the point of transition, the Hillelites considered baptism most important because it portrayed spiritual cleansing and the beginning of a new life."

11

circumcised" (Gen. 17:10). How could Hillel possibly think that baptism was even more important?

He did not explain why he thought so, but there may have been either (or both) of two reasons. First, there is nothing obvious as to the symbolism of circumcision; in fact, it is nowhere explained in the Hebrew Scriptures (what Christians call the Old Testament). There is only one verse in the entire Bible where it is explained at all, Colossians 2:11, where it is called "putting off the body of the flesh." In circumcision, a piece of flesh is, literally, cut off and thrown away.

Baptism, on the other hand, is unmistakable in symbolizing not just a washing away of the past in general, but, more specifically, a washing away of *sin*. When the Jews called people to baptism, it was for *repentance*.

Secondly, Hillel may have been centuries ahead of his time in recognizing the need for a ceremony that applied to women and girls as well as to men and boys. Circumcision was for males only. Baptism was for everyone.

That is, for everyone who wanted to *become* a Jew but who was not born one. The Jews baptized Gentiles who wanted to convert to Judaism. They did not baptize their fellow Jews. The Jews were *already* members of the covenant; they were the children of Abraham. *They* didn't need to be baptized! Baptism was for those "dirty Gentiles."[7]

When we understand that background, John's ministry takes on a very different dimension, for it was precisely this self-understanding of the Jews that he attacked: "You brood of vipers!" he shouted. "Who warned you to flee from the wrath to come? Bear fruit worthy of repentance. *Do not presume to say to yourselves, 'We have Abraham as our ancestor,'* for I tell you, God is able from these stones to raise up children to Abraham. Even now the ax is lying at the root of the trees; every tree therefore that does not bear good fruit is cut down and thrown into the fire" (Matt. 3:7–10).

John called people to *repentance*. And unlike the Jews who preceded

---

7   D. S. Dockery, "Baptism," in *Dictionary of Jesus and the Gospels* (Downers Grove: InterVarsity Press, 1992), 56.

him, he called *all* people to repentance. He also spoke of himself as the forerunner, the one whose ministry was "preparing the way" for one greater than himself, whose sandals, he said, "I am not worthy to untie" (John 1:7).[8]

John was an amazing figure, wearing camel's hair clothing and eating locusts and wild honey! Yet he was anything but comic. Scripture says that all Judea came out to hear him, and we know that he had companies of disciples as far north as modern-day Turkey and as far south as Alexandria, Egypt. He was the Billy Graham of the first century.

When Jesus came to the place where John was baptizing, John identified him as the one greater than himself: "Here is the Lamb of God who takes away the sin of the world! This is he of whom I said, 'After me comes a man who ranks ahead of me because he was before me'" (John 1:29–30).

We have seen that when Jesus asked to be baptized, John was initially reluctant. "Me, baptize you?" he said, in effect. "It ought to be the other way around!" But Jesus insisted this was necessary "to fulfill all righteousness" (Matt. 3:15) and was baptized.

John called people to repentance, warning them of God's anger over their sins. Why, then, did Jesus insist on being baptized? At one point he asked, "Which of you convicts me of sin?" (John 8:46). The Book of Hebrews declares that he was "tempted in every way, just as we are, yet was without sin" (Heb. 4:15, NIV). When they brought Jesus to Pontius Pilate, Pilate said, "I have examined him in your presence and have not found this man guilty of any of your charges against him. Neither has Herod, for he sent him back to us. Indeed, he has done nothing to deserve death" (Luke 23:14–15).If there were any doubt concerning Jesus's innocence at the time of his baptism, God the Father answered it

---

8 This may have been simply an extravagant compliment on the level of, "I am not worthy to be in the same room with him." Or it might have been an intriguing allusion to the "law of Levirate marriage" found in Deuteronomy 25. In the Book of Ruth, the "nearer kinsman" is unwilling to pay the bride price, and Boaz takes off his sandal (3:7–8) and then "takes" Ruth as his wife. John may have been saying that—unlike the nearer kinsman—Jesus *was* willing to pay the bride price, and therefore no one can take off his sandal.

himself by declaring in an audible voice, "This is my Son, the Beloved, with whom I am well pleased" (Matt. 3:17).

John's message was, "God is angry with you because of your sins." God himself declared, "Not this one; with him, I am well pleased."

Why did Jesus insist on being baptized? In effect, *he began his ministry by putting himself in our place*. In *Mere Christianity*, C. S. Lewis commented that a thoroughly evil person could never repent. It takes some spark of goodness, some part of the personality that is responsive to God, to repent at all.

Ironically, the better a person is, the more fully he or she will be able to repent, and "the only person who could do it perfectly would be a perfect person—and he would not need it."[9]

But that is exactly what Jesus did. In submitting to baptism, Jesus was putting himself in the place of sinners and *repenting on their behalf*.

Karl Barth put it this way: "His request was that he should be granted the baptism of repentance as one of the crowd which came to Jordan. He did not set himself over others, but, in expectation of the imminent judgment of God, he set himself in solidarity with them. In this way he not only entered on his office but took the first step on the path which would inevitably end with what took place at Calvary."[10]

A thread running through Jesus's ministry reflects this. At one point, he declared, "I have a baptism to undergo, and how distressed I am until it is completed!" (Luke 12:50, NIV). How could his baptism, at the hands of John, be "incomplete"? There is a clue in Jesus's interchange with his apostles, James and John. When they asked that they might sit beside him in his "glory" (i.e., his kingdom), he replied, "You do not know what you are asking. Are you able to drink the cup that I drink, or be baptized with the baptism that I am baptized with?" (Mark 10:38).

In the Jewish idiom, if something was especially important, it was repeated for emphasis. We read, for instance, in the Psalms: "Bless the Lord, O my soul, and all that is within me, bless his holy name" (Ps.

---

9   C. S. Lewis, *Mere Christianity* (New York: Macmillan, 1972), 59.

10   Karl Barth, *Church Dogmatics*, vol. 4 (Edinburgh: T. & T. Clark, 1958), 258.

103:1). St. Paul wrote to the Philippians: "Rejoice in the Lord always; again I will say, Rejoice" (Phil. 4:4). Jesus so often said, "Truly, truly I tell you…" (or, in the older translation, "Verily, verily I say unto you…").

His double question to the "sons of thunder," James and John, was actually asking the same thing in two different ways. We understand the first question, "Are you able to drink the cup that I drink?" Three times in the Garden of Gethsemane, on the eve of his crucifixion, Jesus prayed, "My Father, if it is possible, let this cup pass from me; yet not what I want but what you want" (Matt. 26:39).

"The cup that I drink" was a cup of suffering and death. "The baptism with which I am baptized" referred to the same thing.

How could Jesus's suffering and death be a baptism? We have now come full circle. If his baptism in the Jordan at the beginning of his ministry was a matter of Jesus putting himself in our place, we remember where he did that most fully and completely: on the cross.

Jesus's ministry, from start to finish, was a matter of his identifying himself with those for whom he came, and it culminated with his taking the burden of sin upon himself and dying in our place. St. Paul said it even more strongly: "For our sake [God] made [Jesus] to *be* sin who knew no sin, so that in him we might become the righteousness of God" (2 Cor. 5:21).

If Jesus's baptism was a matter of his putting himself in *our* place, our baptism is a matter of putting ourselves in *his* place. We are saying that what happened to him was not only *for* us, but it actually belongs *to* us. *His* death was *our* death; *his* resurrection is *our* resurrection.

(The symbolism is more vivid when baptism is done by immersion. The candidate goes into a baptistry or to a river, and the one baptizing "buries" the candidate in the water. He or she is dead and gone. No, wait a moment! The candidate "rises" from the water as a newborn Christian.)

St. Paul says exactly this in his letter to the Romans: "Do you not know that all of us who have been baptized into Christ Jesus were baptized into his death? Therefore we have been buried with him by baptism into death, so that, just as Christ was raised from the dead by the glory of the Father, so we too might walk in newness of life. For if we have been united with him in a death like his, we will certainly be united with him in a resurrection like his" (Rom. 6:3–5).

There is one more piece in this tapestry. Of all the things that John the Baptist might have said regarding Jesus—that he would show us what God is like, that he would perfectly fulfill the commandments, that he would throw open the doors to salvation—the one thing that he did explicitly say was, "He [Jesus] will *baptize you with the Holy Spirit and fire*" (Matt. 3:11).

John implied a great deal in calling Jesus "the Lamb of God who takes away the sin of the world" (John 1:29), but he did not spell that out. The one thing he did say explicitly about Jesus's ministry was that it was Jesus who would be the real Baptizer.

John said, "I baptize you with water for repentance" (Matt. 3:11)—that is, my baptism is symbolic and external—but "Jesus will baptize with the Holy Spirit and with fire." In other words, his baptism is internal, and it is the reality to which mine points.

Thus, Jesus, whose ministry began with his becoming the Anointed One, will have a ministry of baptizing others into that same anointing. It is *almost* to say that everything else that Jesus did, including dying on a cross, rising to new life, and ascending to his Father, was done *so that* he could baptize others as he himself had been baptized. He told his followers, "It is to your advantage that I go away, for if I do not go away, the Advocate will not come to you; but if I go, I will send him to you" (John 16:7).

It is as the ascended Lord that Jesus pours out the Spirit from the Father.

It would be too strong to say that everything Jesus did was so that he could pour out the Spirit because his primary objective was that he might please the Father by winning for us eternal life (John 3:16). But it is not too strong to say that the Anointed One came among us to share that same anointing with us. In the following chapters, we will explore what that entails.

CHAPTER 3

ANOTHER COUNSELOR

"He abides with you and will be in you."

—JOHN 14:17

TOWARD THE END of his earthly ministry, Jesus promised his followers, "I will ask the Father, and he will give you another Counselor to be with you forever—the Spirit of truth. The world cannot accept him, because it neither sees him nor knows him. But you know him, for he lives with you and will be in you" (John 14:16–17, NIV). Other translations say "another Advocate" or "another Comforter." The Greek word is *paraclete,* meaning "one who comes alongside." When Jesus said "another Counselor," he meant "one like me."[11] We are reminded of the passage in Isaiah predicting the coming of the Messiah: "For a child has been born for us, a son given to us…and he is named Wonderful Counselor" (Isa. 9:6).

In effect, Jesus said, "For the past three years, I have been the one enabling your ministry, but shortly I will be returning to the Father. You will not be left on your own; I will ask my Father to send you one like myself who will be with you forever."

He said the disciples *already* know the Holy Spirit (John 14:17). They have already experienced something of his anointing. Jesus sent them out with authority to heal and cast out evil spirits in his name.

---

11   The Greek makes a distinction between "another of the same kind" (*alleilos*) and "another of a different kind" (*heteros*). This is "another of the same kind" (*allon*).

But, he said, they would come to know him in a new way; he will actually live inside them (John 14:17).

Jesus called him "the Spirit of truth." One of the things he said of himself was, "I am the truth" (John 14:6). If Jesus himself *is* the truth, and this Counselor like himself is "the Spirit of truth," we observe the parallel between them.

He said, "the world cannot receive him." In the first chapter of John's gospel, we read that the world "did not receive" Jesus either (John 1:11, NIV).

Jesus then said there were three things in particular that the Holy Spirit would do in the lives of the apostles. First: *"The Holy Spirit, whom the Father will send in my name, will teach you everything, and remind you of all that I have said to you"* (John 14:26).

In doing secular history, the best one could ask for would be the account of eyewitnesses. But that is not enough for the gospel record. The eyewitnesses' recollections will be aided and abetted by the Holy Spirit.

Second: *"When the Counselor comes...he will testify about me. And you also must testify, for you have been with me from the beginning"* (John 15:26–27). After Judas killed himself, Peter suggested to the other apostles that they needed to replace him, and the criterion was that it had to be someone who "accompanied us during all the time that the Lord Jesus went in and out among us, beginning from the baptism of John until the day when he was taken up from one of us" (Acts 1:21–22).[12]

The prerequisite for being numbered among the apostles was having been an eyewitness to the entire ministry of Jesus. But the

---

12 Many have questioned whether the choosing of Matthias was truly God-inspired. It was, after all, *prior* to the outpouring of the Holy Spirit on Pentecost, and there is no indication that there was a word from God that the eleven should do this. And apart from some very unreliable legends, this is the last we ever hear of Matthias. It is arguable that Paul may have been God's choice, which may explain why he contended at such length that he had exercised the ministry of a "true apostle." In Galatians, Paul states that he "did not receive [the gospel] from a human source, nor was I taught it, but I received it through a revelation of Jesus Christ" (Gal. 1:11–12). In effect, Paul claimed to have become an *eyewitness after the fact*, by direct revelation of the gospel. This author knows of no one else in all of history who has made that claim.

eyewitnesses were not going to be alone in giving their testimony. The Holy Spirit would testify to them on his behalf.

Third: *"He will guide you into all the truth; for he will not speak on his own, but will speak whatever he hears, and he will declare to you the things that are to come"* (John 16:13). Jesus said, "I still have many things to say to you, but you cannot bear them now" (John 16:12). It will be the work of the Holy Spirit to complete what Jesus had begun.

So, the Spirit of truth will assist the apostles to *recall* accurately what Jesus has taught them, *interpret* it to them and give them understanding, and *explicate* the meaning of Jesus's deeds and teaching in ways they were not previously able to bear. And, in all this, Jesus said, "He will glorify me, because he will take what is mine and declare it to you" (John 16:14). This is the principal ministry of the Spirit, and everything that he does flows from this purpose.

This may be why the Holy Spirit has often been called "the unknown member of the Trinity." We know about the *God of Israel*, whom Jesus called "Father." What Christians call the Old Testament is the record of his dealings with the Jewish people. We know about *Jesus*, the man who split human history and changed its course forever.

But the ministry of the *Holy Spirit* is to glorify Jesus, to take what is *his* and declare it to us, to remind us of what *he* said and interpret it to us. The Holy Spirit simply does not point to himself.[13]

But there is a pattern of the Holy Spirit appearing and enabling all the way through the Old Testament Scriptures. He was present in the opening words of Genesis, which says "the Spirit of God was hovering over the waters" (Gen. 1:2, NIV). When Genesis says God "breathed" into our first parents, it could be translated he "spirited" into them. In both Hebrew and Greek (and Latin), the same word can be translated "spirit," "wind," or "breath."[14]

When God called Moses to lead his people out of bondage, he

---

13   Sinclair Ferguson wrote, "The assertion that the Holy Spirit, once forgotten, is now forgotten no longer needs rephrasing. For while his *work* has been recognized, the Spirit *himself* remains to many Christians an anonymous, faceless aspect of the divine being." Sinclair B. Ferguson, *The Holy Spirit* (Downers Grove: InterVarsity Press, 1996), 12.

14   Hebrew *ruach*, Greek *pneuma*, Latin *spiritus*

promised to be with him (Exod. 3:12) and "with your mouth and teach you what you are to speak" (Exod. 4:12). When he instructed Moses to appoint elders to help him lead the people, he said, "I will take of the Spirit that is on you and put the Spirit on them" (Num. 11:17). When he instructed Moses to build the Tabernacle, he appointed Bezalel to oversee the construction and said, "I have filled him with the Spirit of God" (Exod. 31:3, NIV).

During the period of the Judges, we read of the Spirit of the Lord "coming upon" successive judges: Othniel (Judg. 3:10), Gideon (Judg. 6:34), Jephthah (Judg. 11:29), and Samson (Judg. 13:25).

When Saul became the first king of Israel, the Spirit of God "possessed him" and he prophesied (1 Sam. 10:10). When Samuel anointed David to become king, the Spirit of the Lord "came mightily upon David from that day forward" (1 Sam. 16:13).

The Old Testament pattern is one of the Holy Spirit "coming upon" or "anointing" or "possessing" the *leaders*—prophets, priests, kings, singers and musicians, warriors—and occasionally those who fit into no category, such as Amos, who said, "I am no prophet, nor a prophet's son; but...the Lord said to me, 'Go, prophesy to my people Israel'" (Amos 7:14).

But the anointing was not for everyone; it was for the few chosen for leadership.

However, in the prophecy of Jeremiah, the Lord said:

> The days are surely coming...when I will make a new covenant with the house of Israel and the house of Judah. It will not be like the covenant I made with their ancestors.... But this is the covenant that I will make with the house of Israel after those days, says the Lord: I will put my law within them, and I will write it on their hearts; and I will be their God, and they shall be my people...for they shall all know me from the least of them to the greatest.
>
> —JEREMIAH 31:31–34

It was exactly this promise that Jesus claimed when he instituted "the new covenant in my blood" (Luke 22:20) and gave us the Supper that celebrates his death on our behalf. In appropriating that promise, he was in effect saying that the birthright of every Christian is to know God through the Holy Spirit with an intimacy as close as that of any of the great heroes of holy history.

So, the Holy Spirit has been active throughout all of history, but Jesus said that he would ask the Father to "send" him in a new and different way. The disciples who had seen him at work and experienced his empowering were actually going to be *indwelt* by him.

Jesus said:

> If I do not go away, the Advocate will not come to you; but if I go, I will send him to you. And when he comes, he will prove the world wrong about sin and righteousness and judgment; about sin because they do not believe in me; about righteousness, because I am going to the Father and you will see me no longer; about judgment, because the ruler of this world has been condemned.
>
> —JOHN 16:7–11

The Holy Spirit will come in a new way. He will come to glorify Jesus. And when he comes, he will convict (or convince) believers that the world completely misunderstands sin, righteousness, and judgment.

Martin Luther said that Jesus went on to give *definitions* of those three words that are radically different from what the world thinks they mean.

The world thinks of *sin* (if it believes in it at all) as "breaking the rules," violating the commandments, doing bad things. But in Jesus's death on the cross, all of those sins are forgiven. The one that remains is the refusal to accept his gift of forgiveness and believe in him.

The world thinks that *righteousness* is the opposite of sin—keeping the rules and doing good things. Jesus said that our righteousness— our right standing before God—is not a matter of what we have done at all; it is a matter of what *he* has done on our behalf!

Jesus completed his work here on earth and went to the Father on our behalf. Our righteousness is his finished work.

(If trust in his finished work is our righteousness, sin is our refusal to believe and trust in that finished work.)

The world thinks that *judgment* is what happens to bad people. Jesus said that judgment happens to the ruler of this world, and it need not fall on anyone else. That is good news! The Holy Spirit glorifies Jesus by convincing people that such good news is true.

The Holy Spirit is the one who makes us alive in Christ. When Jesus told Nicodemus he needed to be born from above, Nicodemus had no idea what Jesus was talking about. It was a play on words when Jesus said, "The wind blows where it chooses, and you hear the sound of it, but you do not know where it comes from or where it goes. So it is with everyone who is born of the Spirit" (John 3:8).

The same wordplay was involved when Jesus appeared in the locked room with his disciples on Easter evening. John records that Jesus greeted them, gave them his peace, showed them his hands and side, and said he was sending them out with the same mission he had been given by the Father. And, "when he had said this, he breathed on them and said to them, 'Receive the Holy Spirit. If you forgive the sins of any, they are forgiven them; if you retain the sins of any, they are retained'" (John 20:22–23).

The scene replayed the creation of our first parents. God breathed—or "spirited"—into them, and he warned them that "in the day" they disobeyed, they would die. That did not happen physically. They disobeyed and lived long lives afterward. But it did happen spiritually. They disobeyed, and the spirit within them died.

The message of the prophets of old was not, "If you sin, you will die." It was, "You are dead in sins and trespasses." Isaiah said, "We are like dead men" (Isa. 59:10). David cried to the Lord, "Create in me a clean heart, O God, and put a new and right spirit within me" (Ps. 51:10). And Jesus said, "You must be born again," and he breathed—or spirited—the Holy Spirit into the apostles, and they became new people in Christ.

It is a kind of theological shorthand to say "I received Christ" or "Christ lives in me." It is his Spirit who comes to indwell the believer. There simply is no other way to be a Christian. St. Paul wrote, "No one can say 'Jesus is Lord' except by the Holy Spirit" (1 Cor. 12:3). He did not mean no one can say those *words*. I knew a famous actor who once played a priest, but he was an atheist himself. He could say the words, but he did not believe them.

St. Paul said that no one can say, as an expression of true conviction, "Jesus is *my* Lord," except by the convincing work of the Holy Spirit. Elsewhere he wrote, "Anyone who does not have the Spirit of Christ does not belong to him" (Rom. 8:9). The connection between Jesus and the Holy Spirit is so close that in the New Testament, he is once called "the Spirit of Jesus" (Acts 16:7), twice called "the Spirit of Christ" (Rom. 8:9; 1 Pet. 1:11), once called "the Spirit of Jesus Christ" (Phil. 1:19), and St. Paul wrote, "God has sent the Spirit of his Son into our hearts" (Gal. 4:6).

In his letter to the Romans, Paul uses the terms "Spirit" and "Christ" almost interchangeably:

> But you are not in the flesh; you are *in the Spirit*, since *the Spirit of Christ* dwells in you. Anyone who does not have *the Spirit of Christ* does not belong to him. But if *Christ is in you*, though the body is dead because of sin, *the Spirit is life* because of righteousness. If *the Spirit of him who raised Jesus from the dead dwells in you*, he who raised Christ from the dead will give life to your mortal bodies also through *his Spirit that dwells in you*.
>
> —ROMANS 8:9–11

Ferguson comments, "Here, clearly, the statements 'Spirit of God lives in you,' 'have the Spirit of Christ' and 'Christ is in you' are three ways of describing the single reality of the indwelling of the Spirit. This complex, multi-layered phenomenon indicates that there is an economic identity between Christ and the Spirit. The Spirit possesses this identity precisely because he was with Christ 'from the beginning' (John 15:27)."[15]

The Spirit's ministry is to glorify Jesus, convince us that Jesus was and is who he claimed to be, and then to begin to make us like Jesus and to equip us for his ministry.

---

15   Ferguson, *The Holy Spirit*, 37.

CHAPTER 4

BETWEEN EASTER
AND PENTECOST

"Stay here in the city."

—LUKE 24:49

FOLLOWING THE RESURRECTION, Jesus appeared to different groups of his disciples in a variety of settings for a period of forty days. He was in a garden...on a road...in a locked room...on the seashore...in Galilee...in Jerusalem.

He appeared to Mary Magdalene, then to the other women, then to Peter, Cleopas and his friend, and the ten apostles (Judas having killed himself and Thomas being away). He made an encore appearance a week later for Thomas. He met with his half-brother James (who previously did not believe in his claims, but who was so thoroughly converted that he became the leader of the Jerusalem church). He appeared to more than five hundred people at one time. He cooked breakfast on a beach. Then he ascended out of this world into another dimension.

All four gospels conclude with Jesus commissioning his apostles to continue Jesus's own ministry of preaching the gospel, baptizing, teaching, and making disciples. But only Luke adds the caveat that Jesus instructed them to "stay here in the city until you have been clothed with power from on high" (Luke 24:49). In hindsight, we know that it turned out to be an additional ten days before the mighty outpouring of the Holy Spirit on the day of Pentecost.

But the disciples did not know how long it would be. Nor did they know exactly what they were waiting for. Jesus merely said, "See, I am sending upon you what my Father promised.... You will be clothed with power from on high" (Luke 24:49). In Acts, Luke recorded that Jesus said, "This is what you have heard from me; for John baptized with water, but you will be baptized with the Holy Spirit not many days from now" (Acts 1:4–5).

So they waited. Luke added that "they were continually in the temple blessing God" (Luke 24:53). What a strange time it had to be!

Everything in the temple worship, everything in the ceremonies and sacrifices pointed toward the coming of a Messiah whom they knew had already come. The priests continually offered sacrifices for sin, and the disciples knew *the* Sacrifice had already been offered. The worshipers asked God to send a Redeemer, and the disciples knew he had already come. The veil of the temple that was rent from top to bottom on Good Friday afternoon would have been repaired immediately; there could not have been a more urgent priority. Yet the disciples knew it had become irrelevant—God had opened the mercy seat to all who will trust in Christ. The high priest continued going about his many duties, but the disciples knew he was already redundant. (There is no point in the stand-in continuing to rehearse when the Star has already finished the show!)

They had to be asking, "What is this power from on high, this baptism in the Holy Spirit? Didn't Jesus breathe the Holy Spirit into us on Easter evening? What more is there?"

We know the details: the mighty rushing wind, the tongues of fire turning the disciples into human counterparts to Moses's burning bush: they were aflame without being consumed or harmed. We know they spoke in languages they had never learned so that all the visitors to the city of Jerusalem (Luke mentions some sixteen different countries they represented) heard them speaking about God in their native languages. We know about Peter's remarkable sermon and the fact that three thousand persons were added to the church that day.

But what is the connection between Jesus breathing on them on Easter evening, saying "Receive the Holy Spirit," and this fantastic rushing wind of God's Spirit fifty days later? There is a direct—and surprising—parallel in the way Passover and Pentecost were connected to each other in the Hebrew Scriptures.[16]

Both Passover and Pentecost were ancient Jewish celebrations long before they were filled with new meaning in Christ. They were two of the three great annual festivals the Jews were commanded to celebrate. (The third was Tabernacles, or Booths, somewhat like Thanksgiving in America; it came in the autumn, a seven-day festival of abundant rejoicing.)

All able-bodied men were to come in person to all three festivals, and many brought their families with them. (We recall Jesus going with his family to the Passover when he was twelve; Luke tells us they made that journey every year [Luke 2:41].)

Passover was the celebration of the Jews' deliverance from bondage following the terrible plagues visited upon Egypt, each worse than the one before, culminating in the death of the firstborn of every Egyptian household. God instructed the Israelites to take the blood of a lamb and splash in on the doorposts and lintels of their homes, and he said, "When I see the blood, I will pass over you, and no plague shall destroy you when I strike the land of Egypt" (Exod. 12:13).

The Last Supper that Jesus celebrated with his apostles was the Passover meal, during which he established the new covenant Jeremiah had promised.[17] He added another deeper dimension to a meal already full of symbolism. The unleavened bread, to be eaten "hurriedly," in

---

16   Many commentators suggest that the Johannine account of Easter evening is simply John's "theological" interpretation of Pentecost. See, for instance, *The New Interpreter's Bible*, vol. 9 (Nashville: Abingdon, 1995), 847–848. This has a degree of plausibility in that John took significant liberties in rearranging the chronology of the synoptics (e.g., his placing the "cleansing of the Temple" at the *beginning* of Jesus's ministry rather than at the *end*, presumably to suggest that his whole ministry was a kind of cleansing of Judaism). But if this were John's account of Pentecost, it would involve not only a different time but a different place, a very different constituency, and a remarkable downplaying of what had to be one of the most dramatic events in the lives of the apostles themselves.

17   We recognize, of course, that John places Jesus's sharing of this "last supper" with his disciples *prior* to the Passover, but all three synoptics state explicitly that it was the Passover meal they shared. (See Matthew 26:19; Mark 14:16; Luke 22:8.)

expectation of deliverance (Exod. 12:11), he said, was his body. The cup of wine, symbolizing the joy of being delivered from slavery, he said, was his blood. He inaugurated an infinitely greater deliverance from an infinitely worse bondage: one of sin, death, and the hell of eternal separation from God.

Pentecost came fifty days after Passover. It was the celebration of the harvest of "First Fruits," the springtime barley crop. In the Middle East, there are two growing seasons, springtime and autumn, with a long, hot, dry summer in between, during which not much can grow. "Pentecost" simply means "the fiftieth day" after Passover. It was also called "the feast of weeks" because there were seven weeks—a "week of weeks," plus the day after the Sabbath on the end—in between these two great festivals.

On the first Christian Pentecost, expatriate Jews had come from all those sixteen nations in obedience to God's command to be in Jerusalem to celebrate this harvest of first fruits. God had promised special blessings to the land and the enlarging of its borders as these celebrations were observed (Exod. 34:24).

But the connection between Passover and Pentecost is more than just the fifty-day interval between them. At the end of the seven-day celebration of the Passover, the people were to go into the barley fields and gather up some of the tiny barley shoots just breaking through the ground, make a sheaf of those shoots, and "raise the sheaf before the Lord" (Lev. 23:11; much as Christians do with their palm branches on Palm Sunday). This was in *anticipation* of the harvest of first fruits that would come fifty days later.

Thus, *Pentecost was contained in embryo in the Passover.* Or, to put it the other way around, *Pentecost completed what began at the end of Passover.*

On the night before he died, Jesus filled the celebration of the Passover with a new dimension of meaning concerning himself. Forever it would now recall his death on our behalf. But on the third day, when God raised him from the dead, he appeared among his disciples and breathed the Holy Spirit into them—just a small breath, like a tender barley shoot.

Fifty days later, the mighty rushing wind of God's Spirit came to transform the one hundred twenty disciples Luke says were "waiting," as Jesus had told them to do, and the three thousand who joined them in baptism after hearing Peter's proclamation. These were the "first fruits" of the Christian "harvest"!

Pentecost looked *backward* to the Passover, but it also looked *forward* to Tabernacles/Booths, sometimes also called "Ingathering." Passover was the harvest of *first* fruits. That very name suggests there will be *more* to be harvested later. The hope was always that a good barley crop would portend a bountiful harvest of all the crops in the autumn.

Tabernacles does not yet have an added Christian dimension or fulfillment, but we have every reason to expect that it will one day. Jesus said, "The harvest is plentiful, but the laborers are few; therefore ask the Lord of the harvest to send out laborers into his harvest" (Matt. 9:37–38). He promised that at the end of this age, there *will* be a harvest when the reapers will "gather my wheat into my barn" (Matt. 13:30).

The Spirit of God anointed Jesus, and his ministry began. Jesus breathed the Spirit of God into his disciples on Easter evening but told them to wait until his Father sent the Spirit in all its fullness so their ministries could begin in a whole new way.

CHAPTER 5

FRUIT . . . MORE FRUIT . . . MUCH FRUIT

"My Father is glorified by this."

—JOHN 15:8

WE HAVE SEEN that the principal ministry of the Holy Spirit is to glorify Jesus. There are three primary ways in which he does this. The first is the convincing, convicting, converting work of bringing people out of unbelief and into faith and new life in Christ. The other two principal dimensions of the Spirit's work in Christian believers are what St. Paul calls *"the fruit of the Spirit"* on the one hand and *"the gifts of the Spirit"* on the other. We need to carefully distinguish these two dimensions of the Holy Spirit's ministry.

First, we are *never* to choose between them. We want (or at least we *should* want) both the fruit and the gifts! The *fruit of the Spirit* is simply the character of Jesus reproduced in his followers: the character traits of disciplined faith.

The *gifts of the Spirit* are specific empowerings in the lives of believers for ministry. St. Paul repeatedly compared the gifts of the Spirit to the different parts of the human body, e.g., "The eye cannot say to the hand, 'I have no need of you'" (1 Cor. 12:21).

Different Christians, just like different parts in the human body, have different functions in the body of Christ, but God has arranged them such that they are mutually dependent upon each other. The pattern is: *different gifts for different Christians.*

Before dealing with the gifts of the Spirit, however, we must consider the fruit of the Spirit. Here the understanding of Scripture is: *all the fruit for all the Christians.*

Jesus called himself the "true vine," and he said his Father is the vine grower and his followers are branches in the vine (John 15:1). He said, "Every branch that bears fruit he prunes to make it bear more fruit.... My Father is glorified by this, that you bear much fruit and become my disciples" (John 15:2, 8). God's desire is fruit...more fruit...much fruit, and Jesus went on to command his disciples to "abide" in his love and to love one another as he loved them.

St. Paul said, "The fruit of the Spirit is love, joy, peace, patience, kindness, generosity, faithfulness, gentleness, and self-control" (Gal. 5:22–23). This is the principal passage on the subject and the only place Paul uses this phrase, but it is not the only place he speaks about such character traits. Paul contrasted the "fruit of the Spirit" with the "works of the flesh," not condemning the physical body per se, but the "works" that flow from our sinful nature even after we have become Christians. From the "flesh" comes every sort of sin and corruption, from envy to drunkenness to murder to adultery (Gal. 5:19–21).

In contrast to the works of the flesh, the fruit of the Spirit is character that is pleasing to God. In this passage, Paul listed nine specific things. As is true with so many biblical lists, it is like buttoning a shirt: start at the top, and if you get the first button right, you will probably get all the rest as well. Get the first one wrong and they will all be wrong! Paul began with love, as did Jesus, and it is as if he said, "Out of love will flow joy, out of joy, peace," and so on.

But it is *fruit,* not *fruits.* It is like a beam of clear, bright, white light hitting a prism: when the light is in the prism and the prism is in the light, we can see the different aspects of the light (interestingly enough, nine colors on the spectrum, as well).[18] When the Christian is in Christ and Christ is in the Christian (through the Holy Spirit),

---

18   Infrared, red, orange, yellow, green, blue, indigo, violet, and ultraviolet.

the different aspects of Christ's character are refracted in and through us. Jesus's own character is the fruit we display through the prism of our individual personalities.

In Colossians 3, Paul discusses the same warfare between "works of the flesh" and "fruit of the Spirit" without using either of those phrases. Here, he gives us another list: compassion, kindness, humility, meekness, patience, bearing with one another, forgiving each other, love, peace, thankfulness, and meditation on the word of Christ (Col. 3:1–17).

That these two lists overlap each other, and there are some characteristics on each that are not on the other, tells us *there is no attempt in either case to give an exhaustive list.* (We will note the same thing when we come to the gifts of the Spirit.)

These are simply some of the character traits of Jesus himself, and theologians have traditionally added truthfulness, modesty, and chastity—and there could be others.

In 1 Corinthians 13, St. Paul discusses the character of *agape* love, and once again, there is a list of character traits that overlaps the other two: love is patient, kind, not envious, not boastful, not arrogant, not rude, not willful, not irritable, not resentful; it does not rejoice in wrongdoing, but rejoices in the truth; it bears all things, believes all things, hopes all things, endures all things, and love never ends (1 Cor. 13:4–7).

There are sixteen synonyms or synonymous phrases in the passage, and nine out of the sixteen are *negative.* (Evidently, then, there are things we need to work on *not* doing toward others.)

Many of these synonyms are also synonyms for *patience* (or they are heavily dependent upon it). One cannot be *kind* without being patient. One cannot *bear all things, believe all things, and endure all things* without being patient. At least eight of the sixteen words or phrases are synonymous with patience.

Extending *agape* love toward someone is at least half a matter of being patient, then. The old phrase, "Please be patient; God isn't finished with me," is really a plea for an expression of Jesus's *agape* love toward each other.

Furthermore, not one of these sixteen characteristics has anything to do with emotions or feelings! There are a lot of feelings in *eros* (thanks be to God). None are essential in *agape*.

In any of these passages, one might substitute the name of Jesus for what is being described. *"Jesus* is patient, kind, not envious..." The character of *Jesus* is "love, joy, peace, patience, kindness..." One of the goals of the Christian life is that his character will be reproduced in us, his followers, and one of the primary ministries of the Holy Spirit is to reproduce that character in us.

In the Colossians passage, the imagery is that of "putting off" and "putting on"—almost exchanging one set of clothes for another: "Do not lie to one another, seeing that you have stripped off the old self with its practices and have clothed yourselves with the new self, which is being renewed in knowledge according to the image of its creator" (Col. 3:9–10).

Twice, Paul effectively told the Colossians, *Because you have already done this, do this.*

- "If with Christ you died..." (Col. 2:20)

- "For you have died..." (Col. 3:3)

- "Put to death, therefore..." (Col. 3:5)

And again:

- "As you therefore received Christ..." (Col. 2:6)

- "You have clothed yourselves..." (Col. 3:10)

- "Clothe yourselves..." (Col. 3:12)

In other words, if one has died to the old self, put the old self to death; if one is alive in a new self, live as a new self. If one has put off the old way of life, put off the old way of life; if one has put on a new way of life, put on a new way of life.

Yes, there is a sense in which Christians are once for all converted, made new, transformed, "born again"; but in another sense, it is a matter of "working out what God has worked in us," and this is an ongoing, daily, moment-by-moment choosing: no, not *that* way; *Jesus's* way. It is enormously practical. The problem is that so much of the time, people treat the fruit of the Spirit as emotions over which they have no control.

People think love is how we *feel* about others.

Bishops receive requests from clergy every month for some of their parishioners to remarry after a divorce. These are accompanied by a letter from the parishioners themselves describing what happened, what they have learned, how they are showing care to former spouses, and so on. Tragically, often the letters say things like, "We stopped loving each other."

What about "love never ends"? (1 Cor. 13:8). *Eros* may have faded; can they not rekindle it with *agape?* If what they had simply ended, then it was not the kind of love the New Testament is talking about!

Agape love is *not* feelings; it is choosing to treat another in a certain way regardless of what our feelings are doing at any given moment. The best cure for feeling a lack of love is *acting* in a loving, caring way.

People think joy is a matter of *enjoying* our circumstances.

But when Paul wrote to the Philippians, "Rejoice in the Lord always; again I will say, Rejoice" (Phil. 4:4), he was under house arrest in Rome, awaiting trial and (as it turned out) execution. He was completely frustrated in terms of his hopes to personally bring the gospel to Britain. Yet he was able to say, in the same passage just eight verses later, "I know what it is to have little, and I know what it is to have plenty. In any and all circumstances I have learned the secret of being well-fed and of going hungry, of having plenty and of being in need. I can do all things through him who strengthens me" (Phil. 4:12–13).

The word *circumstances* comes from two Latin words, *circum*, meaning "around," and *stare*, meaning "to stand." Thus, our circumstances are the things standing around us, and if our joy is dependent on the things standing around us, we are deeply in jeopardy, because sooner or later they are going to fall down and our circumstances will change.

Paul found his joy in the Lord Jesus and in allowing the Holy Spirit to reproduce the joy of the Lord in him. We must ask, in the lists of the fruit of the Spirit—peace, patience, kindness, generosity, and so on—are these going to be determined by circumstances or by the character the Holy Spirit is producing and wants to produce in the followers of Jesus?

We need to work with him, of course. We need to "put off" and "put on." We need to prepare before going into a difficult situation. We need to ask the Lord to manifest himself in and through us.

The Holy Spirit comes to take up residence within the lives of the followers of Jesus so they have his ability to produce the character of Jesus. But they have to "put on" the discipline of adopting the Jesus style. In sanctification, the Holy Spirit is, of course, the dominant partner. It is by the grace of God that we bear fruit. But we are called to cooperate and intend such growth.

Some of the traits that are named as fruit of the Spirit are explicitly *commanded* of us: "*love* your neighbor; *love* your enemy" (Matt. 19:19; 5:43); "*Rejoice* in the Lord always" (Phil. 4:4); "Let the *peace* of Christ rule in your hearts" (Col. 3:15); "Let us run with *patience* the race" (Heb. 12:1, KJV). All of them are at least implicitly commanded, so it is important to remind ourselves that we are not to try to do them in our own strength. They are the *fruit of the Spirit*, enabling Christians to do what God expects.

Jesus said the key to producing "much fruit" is that his followers are to "abide in me, and my words abide in you....If you will keep my commandments, you will abide in my love, just as I have kept my Father's commandments and abide in his love. I have said these things to you so that my joy may be in you, and that your joy may be complete" (John 15:10–11).

This is not a matter of "*earning* our salvation"; it is a matter of *expressing* it. Abiding in him is, among other things, doing what he says—because he says it—expecting him to supply the strength and perseverance to carry it out.

CHAPTER 6

Now Concerning Spiritual Gifts

"To each is given the manifestation of the Spirit for the common good."

—1 Corinthians 12:7

THE HOLY SPIRIT produces fruit—the character traits of Jesus—in the lives of his followers, and we have seen that God's desire is "all the fruit for all the Christians."

When we come to the "gifts of the Spirit," the pattern is very different: "different gifts for different Christians." St. Paul's favorite metaphor for the church is that it is Christ's "body."[19] Like the members of a human body, he says, Christians are mutually dependent upon one another. Just as "the eye cannot say to the hand, 'I have no need of you,' nor again the head to the feet, 'I have no need of you'" (1 Cor. 12:21), so there are two things we cannot and must not say:

- "Because I do not have your gift(s), I am not needed" (1 Cor. 12:15–16).

---

19   Paul also calls the church the "wife" of Christ (Eph. 5:22–33), the "bride" (or "chaste virgin") of Christ (2 Cor. 11:2), a building being constructed upon a foundation (1 Cor. 3:10–15), and runners in a race (1 Cor. 9:24). He frequently refers to Christians as "soldiers" (1 Cor. 9:7; Phil. 2:25; 2 Tim. 2:3; Philemon 1:2), and he tells us to "put on the whole armor of God" (Eph. 6:1ff).

- "Because you do not have my gift(s), you are not needed" (1 Cor. 12:21).

Before discussing the gifts themselves, it is critical that we understand that we are not to choose between the fruit of the Spirit and the gifts of the Spirit. The gifts are given "individually just as the Spirit chooses" (1 Cor. 12:11) to equip God's people to better serve him, each other, and those who do not yet believe. But the *context* within which the gifts are to operate is that of fruit of the Spirit, the character of Christ. It is noteworthy that 1 Corinthians 14 *begins* on exactly the same note on which 1 Corinthians 12 *ends*. First Corinthians 12:31 says, "Strive for the greater gifts. And I will show you a still more excellent way." Then comes the great "love chapter" that says over and over again that if I exercise one or another of the spiritual gifts without doing so in love (first in the catalogue of fruit in Galatians 5), "I am nothing" (1 Cor. 13:2) and "I gain nothing" (1 Cor. 13:3).

First Corinthians 14:1 says, "Pursue love and strive for the spiritual gifts." We could read chapters 12 and 14 as a continuous instruction, leaving out chapter 13 altogether. It is almost as if Paul interrupted himself to say, "I cannot go any further in discussing the gifts of the Holy Spirit without reminding you that they are always and only to be exercised within the context and framework of love."

There are six principal lists of gifts, or manifestations, of the Holy Spirit[20] in the New Testament, and gifts are mentioned individually in numerous other places. The two Greek words translated "gift" are *charisma* (and *charismata*) and *dorea* (with variants *doma* and *dorema*). Some commentators make a distinction between them, saying that *charisma* is an occasional manifestation and *dorea* a developed ministry, or even a recognized office. *Dorea* is used this way in Ephesians 4. But, for the most part, *charisma* and *dorea* are interchangeable.

In the New Revised Standard Version of the New Testament, there are thirty-two different words or phrases naming gifts. Some of them are synonymous with others, or at least partly synonymous. "Ministry"

---

20 Some would say seven by splitting 1 Corinthians 12:27–31 into two lists: verses 27–28 and verses 29–31. Many commentators have failed to notice that, in addition to being a sublime description of love, 1 Corinthians 13 is also a list of the gifts of the Spirit.

is at least partly synonymous with "service" (and both words translate the Greek *diakonia*). One way of "ministering to the saints" is by supporting them financially, i.e., "contributions." "Answered prayer" may be an aspect of the gift of "faith." "Speaking" is a broad category that includes an "utterance of wisdom," an "utterance of knowledge," speaking in "tongues," "interpretation" of tongues, "prophecy," "exhortation," "teaching," and "evangelism." John tells us that when Jesus spoke of the "gift" of "living water," he was referring to the Holy Spirit (John 4:1–30; 7:37–39).

When we place the several lists in columns alongside each other, we will immediately notice that each has some of the gifts on the other lists, but not all of them. Thus it is clear that nowhere is there an exhaustive list of gifts. Each list says, "Here are some of the gifts of the Holy Spirit; these are some of the ways he manifests himself."

In all of the concentration (both positive and negative) on the first great list in 1 Corinthians 12:4–11, many have failed to realize that before chapter 12 is over, a second list appears in the final paragraph. Some commentators actually see two lists in the final paragraph, the first in verses 27 and 28, the second in verses 29 and 30. Paul says, "God has appointed in the church first apostles, second prophets, third teachers…" (1 Cor. 12:27). And then he asks rhetorically, "Are all apostles? Are all prophets? Are all teachers?" (1 Cor. 12:29).

(The answer, clearly, is no. God has appointed *some* to be apostles, not all; *some* to be prophets, not all; *some* to be teachers, not all. The pattern is: *different gifts for different Christians; all the fruit for all the Christians.*)

Let us take a look at the six lists of gifts, side by side, and then we will examine them individually, beginning with the way(s) the gifts listed in 1 Corinthians 12:4–11 functioned in the ministry of Jesus. It is the thesis of this study that Jesus's ministry was an expression of the anointing of the Holy Spirit and the manifestation of his gifts.

And the relevance of that is that he said this same anointing would be ours.

The Anointing of the Spirit—A Comparison of the Lists of Gifts

1 Cor. 12:4–11 (Charisma)	1 Cor. 12:28–31 (Charisma-implied	1 Cor. 13 (Charisma-implied)	Rom. 12:6–8 (Charisma)	Ephesians 4:11 (Dorea)	1 Peter 4:9–11 (Charisma)
Utterance of wisdom			Wisdom (Mysteries)		
Utterance of knowledge			Knowledge		
Faith			Faith		
Healing	Healers				
Working of Miracles	(Doers of) Deeds of power				
Prophecy	Prophets	Prophecy	Prophecy	Prophets	
Discernment (of Spirits)					
Tongues	Tongue-speakers	Tongues			
Interpretation of Tongues	Interpreters				
Often grouped together:	Apostles			Apostles	
REVELATION: wisdom, knowledge, discernment	Teachers		Teaching	Teachers	
	Assistants		Ministry		Service
POWER: faith, healing, miracles	Leaders		Leading		
		Poverty			
INSPIRATION: prophecy,		Martyrdom			
tongues, interpretation			Exhortation		
			Giving		
			Compassion		
				Evangelists	
				Pastors	
					Speaking

Other "Charisma" Verses

2 Cor. 8:4 – ministry to the saints	1 Cor. 7:7, 8 – marriage, singleness
Rom. 6:23 – eternal life	2 Cor. 1:11 – answered prayer

Other "Dorea" Verses

John 4:10 – living water	Romans 5:15 – grace
Acts 2:38 – Holy Spirit	Romans 5:17 – righteousness
Acts 8:10 – Holy Spirit	2 Cor. 9:15 – grace
Acts 11:17 – Holy Spirit	Eph. 3:7 – grace
Heb. 6:4 – Holy Spirit (salvation)	Eph. 4:7 – grace

The list that has received (by far) the greatest attention—and controversy—is in 1 Corinthians 12. Here, Paul refers to nine dramatic and clearly supernatural gifts: the utterance of wisdom, the utterance of knowledge, faith, healing, the working of miracles, prophecy, the discernment of spirits, speaking in tongues, and the interpretation of tongues. These are often grouped together as gifts of *revelation* (wisdom, knowledge, discernment), *power* (faith, healing, miracles), and *inspiration* (prophecy, tongues, interpretation).

The best illustration of most of these gifts is in the ministry of Jesus himself, although we have no definite evidence that he spoke in tongues or interpreted them (more on that in chapter 16).

Recall again his visit to the synagogue in Nazareth at the beginning of his ministry. As we saw in chapter 1, when Jesus read from the prophet Isaiah, he claimed as his marching orders and *raison d'etre* the passage that proclaimed, "The Spirit of the Lord is upon me, *because he has anointed me*" to bring good news, release, and healing (Luke 4:18; Isa. 61:1). It is clear that while Jesus believed that miracles were evidence of his divinity, they were the *manifestation* of his anointing (John 5:36; 10:22–39).

As we examine several episodes in the ministry of Jesus, we will see the gifts of the Holy Spirit in action.

CHAPTER 7

THE UTTERANCE OF WISDOM

"To one is given the utterance of wisdom."
—1 CORINTHIANS 12:8

A LL THREE OF the synoptic gospels show Jesus sparring with the Pharisees and the Sadducees. Both groups were attempting to ensnare him with trick questions. Matthew's account is the fullest, and in it the questions are the most pointed. Matthew has also told us that the Pharisees had already determined to "destroy" Jesus (Matt. 12:14). There was nothing honest about their questions.

"Tell us, then, what you think. Is it lawful to pay taxes to the emperor, or not?" (Matt. 22:17). The tax in question was the head tax or poll tax (*census* in Latin), a denarius, the most widely circulated of which bore the image of Tiberius Caesar and the Latin inscription "Tiberius Caesar, august son of the divine Augustus, high priest."[21] This tax had been imposed in 6 A.D. when Judea became a Roman province, and it provoked the nationalist reaction that eventually became the Zealot movement.[22] Ardent nationalists and most of the common people deeply resented the tax, but the Pharisees and the Herodians supported it because they held their positions only with the support of Rome.

---

21   Daniel J. Harrington, "The Gospel of Matthew," in *Sacra Pagina*, vol. 1 (Collegeville: Liturgical Press, 2007), 310.

22   M. Eugene Boring, "The Gospel of Matthew," in *The New Interpreter's Bible*, vol. 8 (Nashville: Abingdon, 1995), 420.

It was a marvelous trap. If Jesus said yes, he lost ground with the nationalists and commoners. If he said no, he was guilty of sedition.

"Why are you putting me to the test, you hypocrites? Show me the coin used for the tax" (Matt. 12:18). (Owning one was technically a violation of the second commandment against "graven images," and having one in the temple area was considered blasphemous by many of the Jews. Nevertheless, the Pharisees produced a denarius.)

Jesus then asked them, "Whose head is this, and whose title?" They answered, "The emperor's." Then he famously said to them, "Give therefore to the emperor the things that are the emperor's, and to God the thing that are God's." *"When they heard this, they were amazed; and they left him and went away"* (Matt. 22:20–22).

Henry David Thoreau commented that Jesus's answer left them "no wiser than before as to which was which; for they did not wish to know."[23] Actually, he said something a good deal more profound than Thoreau may have realized. If the thing that made the coin Caesar's was the fact that it was made in his image,[24] Jesus was suggesting that while the Jews could legitimately give the tax to the emperor, they were to give to God the thing that was made in *his* image, namely *themselves*.

In any event, the response of the Pharisees was "amazement," and they left him and went away (Matt. 22:22). Mark says they were "utterly amazed at him" (Mark 12:17). Barclay renders it "astonished at the way in which he had parried their question."[25]

It might be supposed that Jesus was simply a naturally (or supernaturally) brilliant person—a great debater—who spotted the trap and avoided it.

But an alternative explanation is that this was an instance of what St. Paul called an "utterance of wisdom," that is, a statement inspired or given by the Holy Spirit that is so provocative it literally confounds the opposition, leaving them speechless. We note it is an *utterance* of wisdom, not just a matter of being wise. It is a word given by God

---

23   "Essay on Civil Disobedience," quoted by George A. Buttrick, *The Interpreter's Bible*, vol. 7 (New York: Abingdon, 1951), 519.

24   *Caesar* and *image* are the words used in the King James Version.

25   Gerard J. Flokstra Jr., *The New Testament Study Bible*, vol. 2 (Springfield: Complete Biblical Library, 1988), 335.

the Holy Spirit in the midst of a particular situation and not one that could have been planned beforehand.

As Matthew continues his account, the evidence favoring this explanation becomes overwhelming. (It will be even clearer when we come to the second gift in the list, the "utterance of knowledge.")

"The same day some Sadducees, who say there is no resurrection, came to him with a question" (Matt. 22:23, NIV). Although their theology differed sharply on many points, the Sadducees were united with the Pharisees in their desire to entrap Jesus. The Sadducees accepted as authoritative only the first five books of the Hebrew Scriptures, and they disbelieved in angels, the overriding providence of God, or the immortality of the soul.[26] Their question was designed to mock Jesus's teaching about heaven and the resurrection.

"Teacher, Moses said, 'If a man dies childless, his brother shall marry the widow, and raise up children for his brother'" (Matt. 22:24). They appealed to the law of "Levirate Marriage" spelled out in Deuteronomy 25:5–10. They told the story of seven brothers, the first of whom married and died childless, leaving his widow to the second, then to the third, and to each in turn, until all seven had married her. Finally, "the woman herself died." (As well she might!) "In the resurrection, then, whose wife of the seven will she be? For all of them had married her" (Matt. 22:28).[27]

Another perfect trap! If she belongs to just one of them, presumably the first, she is being unfaithful with all of the other six. But if she belongs to all of them, they are guilty of adultery, bigamy, and incest. Once again, they thought they had Jesus on the horns of an irresolvable dilemma. And once again, it was a trick question. They knew perfectly well that all of the other brothers had married her in proxy for her first husband.

But Jesus answered them that it is not that one answer or the other is wrong, but he said to them, "*You* are wrong, because you know neither the scriptures nor the power of God" (Matt. 22:29).

---

26 This has prompted more than one wag to say, "This is why they were sad, you see."

27 This may be an allusion to Sarah, the daughter of Raguel, who outlived seven husbands (cf. Tobit 3:8; 6:14).

— With extraordinary brevity, Jesus explicated both halves of his retort, in reverse order. First, the Sadducees do not know the power of God, who raises the dead to a life that is not a mere continuance of this life and its relationships but one that transcends them and in which we are capable of an intimacy with each other that is not dependent upon or limited to the marriage relationship: "For in the resurrection they neither marry nor are given in marriage, but are like angels in heaven" (Matt. 22:30).

Secondly, the Sadducees do not know the Scriptures. Jesus might have cited a number of passages that explicitly teach a coming resurrection (Isa. 25:8; 26:19; Job 19:25–27, Ps. 73:24, 25; or Dan. 12:1–3, for instance), but these were all from books whose authority the Sadducees denied. Instead, he chose the passage in Exodus where God disclosed to Moses his own divine name, *YHWH*, "I am (who I am)." Moses lived perhaps half a millennium after Abraham. When God connected the "I am" name to Abraham, Isaac, and Jacob—"I *am* their God," not "I *was* their God" (when they were living)—he was, in effect, saying, "They are living with me, right now."

Jesus said, "And as for the resurrection of the dead, have you not read what was said to you by God, 'I am the God of Abraham, the God of Isaac, and the God of Jacob'? He is God not of the dead, but of the living" (Matt. 22:31–32).

Matthew's version of the story is nearly identical to Mark's, except that he adds this comment: "And when the crowd heard it, they were astounded at his teaching" (Matt. 22:33). Charles B. Williams renders it, "They were dumfounded at his teaching."[28]

Once again, the opposition was "silenced" (Matt. 22:34) by Jesus's utterance of wisdom.

In Mark's account, Jesus is then approached by a friendly scribe with a question as to which of the commandments is the most important (Mark 12:28). Luke locates the conversation in another part of Jesus's ministry altogether and makes the questioner a lawyer (who

---

28   Charles B. Williams, *The New Testament: A Private Translation in the Language of the People* (Chicago: Moody Press, 1960), 61.

answers his own question [Luke 10:25–37]). But Matthew makes it part of the continuing attempt to entangle Jesus: "*When* the Pharisees heard that he had silenced the Sadducees, they gathered together, and one of them, a lawyer, asked him a question *to test him.* 'Teacher, which commandment in the law is the greatest?'"

Perhaps the lawyer's intention was to get Jesus to single out one commandment *at the expense of the others.* But when Jesus answered by *summarizing* all of the laws into two—"the Great Commandment" and "a second like it" (Matt. 22:37–40)[29]—Jesus evidently *passed the test,* as there was no rebuttal or further discussion. Once again, silence.

Jesus quoted two positive commandments from the Torah: "You shall love the Lord your God" and "love your neighbor as yourself" (from Deuteronomy 6:5 and Leviticus 19:18). Daniel Harrington commented, "If there is any originality in Jesus' answer it lies in the combination of these two commandments."[30]

The Pharisees tried twice, the Sadducees once, and three times in a row, Jesus's answers silenced the opposition. Now it was his turn to ask them (the Pharisees) a question: "What do you think of the Messiah? Whose son is he?" (Matt. 22:41). The Pharisees gave the standard Jewish answer: "The son of David" (Matt. 22:41). Passages such as Jeremiah 23:5 ("The days are surely coming, says the LORD, when I will raise up for David a righteous Branch") and Isaiah 11:1, 10 ("A shoot shall come out from the stump of Jesse…the root of Jesse," i.e., David's father) had well established this expectation.

Jesus's further question hinged upon two presuppositions. First, David wrote Psalm 110, and second, no one can ever attain greater status than one's ancestors (which is why we never "outgrow" the commandment to honor our parents). We were literally contained in their loins. What they did affects us.[31]

Jesus asked them, "How is it then that David by the Spirit calls him [the Messiah] Lord, saying, 'The Lord said to my Lord, "Sit at

---

29 "A second is like it" is unique to Matthew.

30 Harrington, "The Gospel of Matthew," 316.

31 St. Paul's argument about "original sin" in Romans 5 is based in part upon this understanding.

my right hand, until I put your enemies under your feet.'" If David thus calls him Lord, how can he be his son?" (Matt. 22:43–45).

In the Hebrew text it is "the LORD" (*YHWH*) who speaks to "my Lord," understood by the Jews to be the future Messiah. (This distinction is not reflected in the Greek text where *kyrios* is used in both instances, but Jesus's hearers certainly would have known which was which.)

Jesus was not, of course, denying that the Messiah would be the *biological* descendant of David; he was suggesting that the Messiah had to be *more* than just that—he would have to be, in truth, the very Son of God.

Once more, Matthew adds a stronger commentary than is found in Mark: "No one was able to give him an answer, nor from that day did anyone dare to ask him any more questions" (Matt. 22:46).

Dennis and Rita Bennett said this:

> *The supernatural gift of the "word of wisdom"* is the sudden and miraculous giving of wisdom to meet a particular situation, or answer a particular question, or utilize a particular piece of knowledge, natural or supernatural. Like the "word of knowledge" it is not a human ability at all, but the sheer gift of God. It would be difficult to say whether wisdom or knowledge is the more important. It would be rather like trying to decide which is the more important, the paint, or the painter, for whereas the artist can't paint a picture without the materials, the materials without the person who knows how to use them can be a source of damage and ugliness.[32]

Four times in a row, Jesus silenced the opposition with his brilliant answers and questions. As we turn our attention to the second of the gifts of the Spirit, the utterance of knowledge, the evidence will become more compelling that this brilliance was, in fact, an expression of the anointing of the Holy Spirit.

---

32   Dennis and Rita Bennett, *The Holy Spirit and You* (Plainfield: Logos International, 1971), 163.

CHAPTER 8

THE UTTERANCE OF KNOWLEDGE

"To another the utterance of knowledge."

—1 CORINTHIANS 12:8

JESUS'S INTERCHANGE WITH the woman of Samaria at Jacob's well is a fascinating illustration of his speaking a "word" or "utterance" of knowledge. To her complete surprise, he engaged her in conversation. He was a Jew and she a Samaritan, and ancient hostilities between these two neighboring peoples had all but prescribed that "Jews have no dealings with Samaritans" (John 4:9, RSV). Secondly, he was a man and she a woman, and they had not been introduced. And thirdly, as the story unfolds, we discover she had a shady personal history, which was why, presumably, she came to draw water from the well in the middle of the day. Most people would come in the cool of the morning or evening. She evidently came in the heat of midday to avoid social contact and the risk of being snubbed.

William Barclay commented that the well in question "was more than half-a-mile from Sychar where she must have stayed and there was water there. May it be that she was so much of a moral outcast that the women even drove her away from the village well and she had to come here to draw water?"[33]

So, on no less than three counts, she was startled when Jesus asked

---

33   William Barclay, *The Gospel of John*, vol. 1, revised ed. (Louisville: Westminster, 1975), 148.

her for a drink. "How is it that you, a Jew, ask a drink of me, a woman of Samaria?"[34] Jesus tantalized her with his mysterious response: "If you knew the gift of God, and who it is that is saying to you, 'Give me a drink,' you would have asked him, and he would have given you living water" (John 4:10).

In a later reference to "living water," John tells us Jesus was speaking about the Holy Spirit (John 7:39), but at this point the woman assumed he was speaking of drinking water, and Jesus claimed the water he offered would permanently satisfy her thirst. She responded, "Sir, give me this water, so that I may never be thirsty or have to keep coming here to draw water" (John 4:15).

Jesus asked her to call her husband, and she responded, "I have no husband" (John 4:17). Jesus said to her, "You are right in saying, 'I have no husband'; for you have had five husbands, and the one you have now is not your husband. What you have said is true" (John 4:17–18).

We might wish we could hear Jesus's tone of voice and see his facial expressions, but all we have are his words. But as the conversation unfolds, it is hard to imagine him speaking in judgment or condemnation. More likely there was a gentle, quizzical smile on his face as he said, in effect, "You dear, loveable fraud: you are coming here in the middle of the day, half a mile farther than you need to go to find water because your neighbors consider you the town tramp, little better than a harlot. But, yes, you have told me the truth. You do not have a husband now. You have had five so far, and you are currently living with a boyfriend 'in sin,' but that is technically the truth."

The question is, how did Jesus know that? Do we suppose he stopped by the courthouse to examine the records before his chance encounter with this woman? Of course not. *The utterance of knowledge is a matter of articulating something given to us immediately by the Holy Spirit, without prior knowledge of it.*

John Wimber defined the gift of knowledge as "the supernatural revelation of facts about a person or situation, which is not learned

---

34   Ibid.

through the efforts of the natural mind, but is a fragment of knowledge freely given by God, disclosing the truth which the Spirit wishes to be made known concerning a particular person or situation."[35]

In this woman's case, it was life-changing. First, she recognized Jesus as a prophet (John 4:19). Then she questioned whether he was, indeed, the Messiah (John 4:29). And she ran back into town to tell the very people she had been avoiding, "Come and see a man who told me everything I have ever done!" (John 4:29).

Of course he had not told her *everything* she had ever done. But Jesus touched this woman at her most vulnerable point: she had gone from relationship to relationship and from bed to bed, seeking something that eluded her. And here was someone who knew that, who did not condemn her for it, and who actually invested her with the dignity of having something to give him: a drink of water, though she was a woman, a Samaritan, a tramp, and they had not been introduced. It so converted her that she became, in effect, the first evangelist to the Samaritans.

Another incident at the very beginning of Jesus's ministry involved a similar utterance of knowledge. Jesus called Philip to be one of his followers, and Philip in turn told Nathanael, "We have found him about whom Moses in the law and also the prophets wrote, Jesus son of Joseph from Nazareth" (John 1:45). Nathanael skeptically replied, "Can anything good come out of Nazareth?" (John 1:46). Rather than arguing, Philip told Nathanael to see for himself.

Jesus saw Nathanael coming to him and said of him, "Behold, an Israelite indeed, in whom [there] is no guile" (John 1:47, RSV).

The whole encounter is a play on the story of the patriarch Jacob who wrestled with the angel of God and would not let go until he blessed him.[36] Jacob, whose name meant "supplanter," is the only man in the Scriptures who was said to have come "with guile" when he tricked his father Isaac into giving him the blessing that should have

---

35   Cited by David Pytches, *Come, Holy Spirit* (London: Hodder and Stoughton, 1985), 99.

36   Genesis initially called him a "man," but after the blessing, Jacob/Israel said, "I have seen God face to face" (Gen. 32:30).

been his brother Esau's, having previously persuaded Esau to trade his birthright for a bowl of stew.[37]

When Jacob refused to let go until the angel blessed him, the angel said to him, "You shall no longer be called Jacob, but Israel, for you have striven with God" (Gen. 30:28). The name *Israel* literally means "the one who strives with God" or, simply, "God strives."

Jacob wrestled with (the angel of) God until the guile was taken out of him and his name was changed to Israel, and Jesus greeted Nathanael as "a true Israelite in whom there is no guile." He went on to say, "You will see heaven opened and the angels of God ascending and descending upon the Son of Man" (John 1:51), clearly a reference to Jacob/Israel's dream of the ladder (or stairway or ramp) reaching from earth to heaven with the angels of God ascending and descending upon it (Gen. 28:10–17). In effect, Jesus was saying to Nathanael, "I am that ladder."

But first we must note Nathanael's astonishment at Jesus's greeting, "Behold, an Israelite indeed, in whom is no guile!" Nathanael said to him, "How do you know me?" (No modesty there, false or otherwise!) Jesus answered him, "Before Philip called you, when you were under the fig tree, I saw you." Nathanael answered him, "Rabbi, you are the Son of God! You are the King of Israel!" (John 1:47–49).

In all of history, has there ever been a more sudden or dramatic conversion? In *four verses* Nathanael goes from complete skepticism ("Can anything good come out of Nazareth?") to unqualified conviction ("You are the Son of God...the King of Israel!") And all it took was Jesus saying, "I saw you under the fig tree."

We can only wonder what in the world he was doing there! Two possibilities come to mind. Nathanael *might* have been doing something that demonstrated he was precisely what Jesus said he was, a true and guileless Israelite (although we might wonder what could demonstrate that!).

On the other hand, this could be another instance of Jesus gently calling Nathanael a fraud, just as he did the woman at the well.

---

37   Cf. Genesis 27:1–38 and Genesis 25:29–34, respectively.

Rabbinic students would often pray and meditate under fig trees. It is just possible that whatever Nathanael was doing under that fig tree was just the opposite of what he should have been doing there![38]

In any event, the thing that abruptly converted Nathanael was the fact that Jesus saw him doing whatever he was doing, when he had supposed that he was doing it in secret. That Jesus "saw" him, and told him so, was an utterance of knowledge. Jesus knew something supernaturally because the Holy Spirit revealed it to him, and saying so converted the skeptic Nathanael.

How did Jesus receive these words of wisdom and knowledge? We are not told; we simply see the evidence that he did so. Perhaps some illustrations of "ordinary folks" receiving similar gifts from God will shed light on the matter.

Tom Riley, president of "Faith Alive!" a renewal ministry in the Episcopal Church, recounted the following story:

> Our daughter, Jennifer, is the mother of three and a teacher at a Christian school in Lawrenceville, Georgia, about a 45-minute drive north of Atlanta. She called me in mid-December [2008] to tell me her adventure that morning, advising that she often includes in her morning prayers, "Lord, send me someone to minister to."
>
> Daddy, as I was driving Emily (their youngest) to school, I had this vision. It was the face of a young black woman. I couldn't get this face out of my mind. It was so very clear. After I dropped off Emily and started to drive home, the face faded and I felt this urgent message, "Rescue Atlanta!"
>
> [Jennifer said it kept repeating in her mind. ("Rescue Atlanta? I can't rescue Atlanta! I don't think it needs rescuing.") But she went home and Googled it on the Internet, discovering that Rescue Atlanta is a feeding program in the inner city.]
>
> So I canceled the luncheon that I had planned on attending, explaining that something important had come up. I baked some cookies and drove into a kind of spooky part of Atlanta, finally locating a warehouse set up for feeding the homeless.

---

38   One might imagine a contemporary seminarian having a *Playboy* magazine hidden inside a textbook, for instance.

After dropping off the cookies, I visited awhile and was leaving when I saw a black woman entering the warehouse—the same black woman I had seen in my vision. I sat down beside her and said, "I believe God has sent me to encourage you and to tell you that he loves you and he is walking with you."

The woman began to weep and said, "I've had a tough life." Jennifer responded, "I know. Your mother and father were killed when you were just a baby." The woman—and Jennifer—were astounded. "How did you know?" Jennifer said, "I didn't know. God just this minute told me, to prove to you that he is here right now. You do have a wonderful Father and he loves you."

Jennifer discovered that the woman was about to make a major change in her lifestyle, a new approach to making money. She encouraged the woman to stay the course and that her Father was near. They hugged, prayed together, and Jennifer drove home praying for Tammy, who had shared so much of her life and temptations.[39]

My Meeting with Stuart

When I was in college, I used to visit a small Episcopal church across the street from campus to pray and meditate, usually in the evenings, when I could be alone in the building. One night a man was playing the organ in the choir loft when I entered. My first impulse was to leave and come back some other time. But for whatever reason, I decided to ignore him and go pray at the altar rail.

As I prayed, I had a profound sense that the Lord was saying to me, "Go pray with that man." I tried to dismiss it, but I could not. So I went up into the loft and waited until he finished the piece he was playing. "Would you pray with me?" I asked. "Of course," he said.

Now what? I simply continued my own personal prayers, and when I finished, he said, "Amen." We introduced ourselves: his name was Stuart, and he told me he was a medical technician from the next town who was taking organ lessons from the church organist, and she allowed him to practice in the church.

---

39   Tom Riley, personal e-mail sent to the author, May 5, 2009. Used with permission.

I left the church thinking to myself: he must be wondering what in the world that was about! (As was I!)

He told me months later that when he got home that evening, he got his mother's Bible out of the bookcase, and he opened at random to the first chapter of the fourth gospel, where he read, "There was a man sent from God, whose name was John" (John 1:6).

Two nights later, I had occasion to return to the church to pray about a retreat I was responsible for coordinating the following Saturday. Stuart was there again, and as I walked down the aisle, I had an even stronger sense that the Lord was prompting me to say something to him: "Stuart, you're going on a retreat this Saturday!"

"Oh, I'd love to," he said, "but I have a friend coming to visit for the weekend."

To my astonishment, I heard myself saying, "Your friend will not be able to come." Stuart replied, "If he doesn't, I'll go on your retreat." The next night he telephoned: "My friend just called, and he cannot come. Where do I meet you on Saturday?" Like Jennifer in the previous story, I do not know how I knew; I just knew.

But also like Jennifer, I had to take the risk of acting on what I sensed was a word from God. I had to speak it out and be thought foolish (and possibly be proven wrong).

At the retreat on Saturday, our speaker explained the gospel with great clarity and persuasiveness, and when there was a time for testimonies in the afternoon, Stuart said, "I guess I am the newest, so I will go first." He said that at the break, the retreat leader had prayed with him, and he had given his life to Christ.

The following week I received a note in the mail. Stuart wrote, "I have been asking God all week what he wants me to do with my life, and tonight he spoke to me. He is asking me to become a medical missionary."

Stuart quit his job, took his savings, and enrolled in classes at Columbia Bible College, got ordained as a Baptist minister, and spent the next thirty years of his life as a medical missionary working with Wycliffe Bible Translators in Peru.

He was the best man in my wedding. The Book of Hebrews says,

"Jesus Christ is the same yesterday and today and forever" (Heb. 13:8). Evidently that can be said of the Holy Spirit, as well. He gives gifts for ministry, and among them is the utterance of knowledge.

CHAPTER 9

Faith, Part One

"To another faith."

—1 Corinthians 12:9

J UST AS THE "word" or "utterance" of wisdom is more specific than simply being wise, and just as the "word" or "utterance" of knowledge is more specific than simply being widely knowledgeable, so "faith," when it is listed as one of the gifts of the Spirit, is something more specific than the general saving faith which is shared by all believers.

Bishop David Pytches makes the very helpful distinction:

> There are four kinds of faith in the New Testament.
> 1. There is faith which is a *creed*—the doctrine we profess to believe (Eph. 4:13; 1 Tim. 6:20–21; Jude 3).
> 2. There is faith which is the basic *trust* which one has in God for salvation (John 3:16; Eph. 2:8; Heb. 11:1–5).
> 3. There is faith which is a *fruit* of the Spirit—a loyalty which is produced by the Holy Spirit and cultivated by the believer, i.e., faithfulness (Gal. 5:22).
> 4. There is a faith which is a *gift* of the Spirit—a mountain-moving surge to which both Jesus and Paul refer (Matt. 17:20; 21:21 and 1 Cor. 13:2).[40]

---

40   Pytches, *Come, Holy Spirit*, 109.

Saving faith is one of the great themes of Scripture in general and the New Testament in particular. The writer to the Hebrews states unequivocally, "Without faith it is impossible to please God" (Heb. 11:6), and he goes on to give a rudimentary definition of the term as he uses it. Faith is a matter of believing "that [God] exists and that he rewards those who seek him" (Heb. 11:6).

In his letter to the Galatians, Paul says that we Christians "have come to believe in Christ Jesus, so that we might be justified by faith in Christ" (Gal. 2:16). In Ephesians, he declares that this saving faith "is not of [our] own doing; it is the gift of God—not the result of works, so that no one may boast" (Eph. 2:8–9). In Romans, he seems to acknowledge that some have stronger or bolder faith than others: we are to "think with sober judgment, each according to the measure of faith that God has assigned" (Rom. 12:3).

But when Paul lists faith as one of the gifts or manifestations of the Spirit in 1 Corinthians 12, and when we recall that the whole structure of the argument there are "different gifts for different Christians,"[41] we discover he is referring to something more focused than general saving faith.

Charles Hummel put it this way:

> The gift of faith, exercised by some, designates the confidence in a specific situation that God is about to act. It is often the assurance that God is working through me—the one gifted with faith.[42]

Bishop Pytches put it similarly:

> This gift is a supernatural surge of confidence from the Spirit of God which arises within a person faced with a specific situation or need whereby that person receives a transrational certainty and assurance that God is about to act through a word or action. This miracle utterance covers creation or destruction, blessing or

---

41   Paul's repeated point is "varieties of gifts...varieties of services...varieties of activities...to one this, and to another that" (1 Cor. 12:4–11).

42   Charles E. Hummel, *Fire in the Fireplace: Contemporary Charismatic Renewal* (Downers Grove: InterVarsity Press, 1978), 132.

cursing, removal or alteration. "It is both the irresistible knowledge of God's intervention at a certain point and the authority to effect his intervention through the power of the Holy Spirit" (Grossman).[43]

Once again, our best illustrations are in the ministry of Jesus. When Jesus cursed a certain fig tree for being fruitless, the disciples were "amazed." "How did the fig tree wither at once?" they asked. Jesus answered them, "Truly I tell you, if you have faith and do not doubt, not only will you do what has been done to the fig tree, but even if you say to this mountain, 'Be lifted up and thrown into the sea,' it will be done. Whatever you ask for in prayer with faith, you will receive" (Matt. 21:18–22).

In Mark's version of the story, "ask for in prayer with faith" is expanded to "whatever you ask for in prayer, *believe that you have received it*, and it will be yours" (Mark 11:24).

No doubt these passages have caused great consternation for many, for they have attempted to exercise faith regarding some specific need and their attempts have been futile. Some have attempted to convince themselves they have "received" something before they have actually done so, and in the end they have been deeply disappointed.

Indeed, a whole school of "Faith Teaching" evolved in the midtwentieth century. Some of its mantras were (and in some cases still are): "Name it and claim it," "Believe it, receive it," "What you say is what you get," "Doubt it and go without it." The problem, of course, is that if it is a "gift," it is not a matter of effort on our part. We cannot manufacture the kind of faith needed for specific prayers to be answered.

But note the point: "faith" in this regard concerns believing God for *some specific need*. It is *not* a matter of general "saving faith," but of *God giving some people in some specific circumstances the faith to believe him for some specific things.*

A careful study of the twenty-six healing miracles of Jesus that are recounted in the Gospels reveals a number of fascinating points. First,

---

43 Pytches, *Come, Holy Spirit*, 109.

in many of them—*but not all*—Jesus commends the faith of the recipient.[44] In some instances, he commends the friends or relatives of the recipient.[45] But in some cases, there is no mention of anyone's faith (other than that of Jesus himself, perhaps, though this is never mentioned, but it may be inferred).[46]

Secondly, the gifts of the Spirit often work in tandem with each other. As we have just noted, many of the "miracles of healing" were accompanied by God giving to someone (the recipient, his or her parents, the recipient's friends) a gift of faith to believe for that healing. It is often difficult to determine where one gift leaves off and another begins.

Thirdly, while faith is not always explicitly mentioned as a prerequisite for healing or other miracles, we have already noted that the *lack* of faith can be a limiting or hindering factor. When Jesus returned to his hometown, "he could do no deed of power there, except that he laid his hands on a few sick people and cured them" (Mark 6:5).

Once, after a full day of teaching, Jesus and the apostles started across the Sea of Galilee. In his exhaustion, Jesus fell asleep on the cushion in the stern of the boat. Meanwhile, "a great windstorm arose," creating huge waves that threatened to swamp the boat. The apostles awakened him in fear: "Teacher, do you not care that we are perishing?" Jesus "rebuked" the wind and commanded the sea to be still and at peace, and it was so—"a dead calm."[47] Then he said to the apostles, "Why are you afraid? Have you still no faith?" And they were awestruck, saying to one another, "Who then is this, that even the wind and the sea obey him?" (Mark 4:35–41).

Jesus's double question is usually taken to mean, "Why are you afraid, when I am in your midst? Have you no faith *in me*?" If that is what he meant, it is still consistent with the point we are observing, namely, that "faith" in this context means believing God—or in this

---

44   E.g., Matt. 9:22; 9:29; Luke 18:42

45   E.g., Matt. 8:10; 15:18; Luke 5:20

46   E.g., Matt. 12:9–14; Mark 1:29–31

47   Jesus's rebuke (*epetimesen*) of the wind and his command that the sea be calm is a direct parallel to his rebuke and exorcism of demons (Mark 1:25; 3:11; 9:25).

instance, believing that Jesus was believing God—for a specific need (stilling the storm and saving the lives of the apostles).

But when the passage is read in context, there may be another meaning altogether. On this particular day of teaching, every parable and illustration that Mark records has to do with growing, developing, and exercising the gift of faith in the word, power, and reign of God so that when the "storm" comes, the followers of Jesus will be equipped to exercise the gift of faith to calm the storm themselves.

Jesus began with the parable of the sower, and when he was "alone...with the twelve," he told them this parable was foundational to understanding all the others (Mark 4:13). The seed being sown is the Word of God (Mark 4:14). The purpose of sowing this seed is that it will take root, flourish, and produce a harvest of thirty, sixty, or a hundredfold (Mark 4:20). The issue is the condition of the soil on the one hand and the desire of Satan to prevent good growth on the other.

The parable does not say this, but the implication is inescapable: the followers of Jesus must be prepared to defend themselves against Satan taking away the word that is sown, and they must do what they can to tend to the soil of their lives and those of others—to remove their "rocky" hardness of heart and cut back the thorns and weeds that would choke the good growth of God's Word in their lives (fear of persecution, the cares of this world, and the desire for other things).

Then the Word of God will flourish in the life of the believer, and, as Paul puts it to the Romans, "So faith comes from what is heard, and what is heard comes through the word of Christ" (Rom. 10:17). (That is not a *specific* gift of faith for a *specific* situation, but it would seem to be preparatory for receiving such a gift from God, should he choose to give it.)

Jesus then told the parable of the lamp under the bushel basket, instructing the disciples to "Listen!" and once again promising growth in faith: "For to those who have, more will be given; and from those who have nothing, even what they have will be taken away" (Mark 4:21–25). Elsewhere he developed the same theme of the parable of the talents (Matt. 25:14–30; Luke 19:11–27). In both cases, he was saying, in effect, "Use what you have been given and it will grow; ignore it and it will wither away."

Similarly, in the parable of the growing seed (Mark 4:26–29) and the parable of the mustard seed (Mark 4:30–32), Jesus taught that if we give God's Word a chance, it will produce a harvest of faith in our lives: "First the stalk, then the head, then the full grain in the head" (Mark 4:28), and again, the mustard seed "will become the greatest of all shrubs" (Mark 4:32).

Elsewhere Jesus explicitly identified the mustard seed as the iconic symbol of the kind (and amount) of faith needed to move a mulberry tree (Luke 17:6), or even a mountain (Matt. 17:20–21). In Matthew's gospel, Jesus upbraided the disciples for their inability to exorcize an epileptic boy, saying it was because of their "little faith" (Matt. 17:20–21),[48] and then added, "If you have faith the size of a mustard seed, you will say to this mountain, 'Move from here to there,' and it will move; and nothing will be impossible for you" (Matt. 17:20–21).

But perhaps Jesus was intending not only a *rebuke*, but an *encouragement*, as well: "Moving a mountain would *only* require 'faith the size of a mustard seed'; if you lack even that, ask God to give it as the gift of faith for that specific situation." Sometimes faith needs to grow. Sometimes that takes time.

HOW A SEED CAN GROW

When I was twelve years old, my family moved into a new home in Connecticut. The backyard had not been mowed for some time, and my father asked me to help clear it. Hidden in the weeds was a large boulder (one of several in the neighborhood said to have been brought there by glacial movement in one of the Ice Ages). Growing from a tiny crack in the boulder was a thin green shoot.

---

48   In calling the boy an epileptic, his father seems to be naming a medical condition: "I brought him to your disciples, but they could not cure him" (Matt. 17:16). But Jesus treated it as an instance of demonic affliction; He "rebuked the demon, and it came out of him" (Matt. 17:18). We will examine the difference between healing and exorcism in chapter 15.

I was about to remove it with a weed whacker when my father said, "No, don't do that. That's an oak."

How an acorn got into that crack, took root, and drew nourishment remains unknown. But I visited that property more than a half-century later and found a twisted, gnarled, mighty oak tree growing in the midst of the shattered pieces of what used to be a great boulder. It simply took time for the acorn to do its work.

Clearly there is a difference between faith that takes time to grow and the sudden gift of unexpected certainty that God is about to do something wonderful, or even that we can do something in the power of his Spirit. But at the same time, the two must be related if Jesus could be so often disappointed when his followers failed to have—or use—faith in situations of specific need.

So, was it the (eventual) strength and size of the mustard tree that Jesus was likening to the exercise of faith? Or was it the persistence of a tiny seed growing into "the greatest of all shrubs" (Mark 4:31–32)?

Either way, we have come full circle. In a day of teaching that left Jesus so exhausted that he could sleep through a storm threatening to capsize the boat, Jesus was not talking only about faith in general, but also about the kind of faith that can move mountains: faith which is a gift of the Spirit, which we will be much more ready to receive if we have carefully tended the soil of our lives.

Mark says, "With *many* such parables [Jesus] spoke the word to them, as they were able to hear it; he did not speak to them except in parables, but he explained everything in private to his disciples" (Mark 4:33–34). In other words, the day's teaching did not consist of only the parables Mark (and Matthew) recorded, but many additional parables on the same subject. No wonder Jesus was exhausted at the end of the day!

Perhaps his double question in the boat that evening was a kind of pop quiz after the day of teaching. "Why are you afraid? Have you learned nothing today? Have you no faith *that you could still this storm?*"

Jesus continually exhorted his followers to *use* their faith.[49] He was

---

49   E.g., Matt. 21:21; Luke 17:6

often saddened, and sometimes angry, when they failed to do so.[50] Frequently he was surprised and delighted when someone *did* use his or her faith.[51]

In the feeding of the five thousand, John tells us that Jesus's question to Philip, "Where are we to buy bread for these people to eat?" was asked "*to test him*, for [Jesus] himself knew what he was going to do" (John 6:5–6). But how could this have been a test unless Jesus was hoping that Philip and the others had learned enough, by this time, to multiply the loaves (by faith) themselves? In Mark's version of the same story, Jesus instructed the disciples to do precisely that: "*You* give them something to eat" (Mark 6:37).

When the disciples were unable to exorcise the demoniac boy, Jesus said it was due to their lack of faith (Matt. 17:20), and some of the texts add, "But this kind does not come out except by prayer and fasting,"[52] suggesting that at least sometimes the gift of faith may thus be strengthened.

Small beginnings coupled to persistence is one of the great themes of the kingdom of God: mustard-seed faith, a little leaven, the widow's mites, faithfulness in small things, five loaves and two fish, two or three gathered in his name, ten talents, five talents, one talent—it is not how much we have, it is what we do with what we have.

Jesus had the faith to command even the elements to obey him, and it was his desire to see his followers have the same kind of faith as the Holy Spirit gifted them with faith in specific situations.

---

50   E.g., Matt. 6:30; 8:26; 14:31; 16:8; 17:20

51   E.g., Matt. 8:10; 9:2, 22, 29; Mark 5:34; 10:52; Luke 5:20; 7:9, 50; 8:48; 17:19; 18:42

52   Matt. 17:21, in some ancient authorities.

CHAPTER 10

Faith, Part Two

"Ask in faith."

—James 1:6

THE GIFT OF faith is so integrally related to the working of other gifts of the Holy Spirit that we must take a second look at it.

We noted earlier[53] that in the Jewish idiom, if something is very important it is repeated, sometimes in slightly different phraseology, e.g., "O magnify the Lord with me, and let us exalt his name together" (Ps. 34:3). In the latter chapters of John's Gospel, Jesus repeats an astonishing promise to his followers no less than six times in a row:

- "Very truly, I tell you, the one who believes in me will also do the works that I do and, in fact, will do greater works than these, because I am going to the Father. *I will do whatever you ask in my name,* so that the Father may be glorified in the Son" (John 14:12–13).

- *"If in my name you ask me for anything, I will do it"* (John 14:14).

- "If you abide in me, and my words abide in you, *ask for whatever you wish, and it will be done for you"* (John 15:7).

---

53 See chapter 2.

- "You did not choose me but I chose you. And I appointed you to go and bear fruit, fruit that will last, so that *the Father will give you whatever you ask him in my name*" (John 15:16).

- "Very truly, I tell you, *if you ask anything of the Father in my name, he will give it to you*" (John 16:23).

- *"Ask and you will receive,* so that your joy may be complete" (John 16:24).

Five out of the six times, Jesus specifies that we are to ask "in his name," and once he stipulates that we are to "abide" (Gk. *meinete*) in him and that his words must "abide" (Gk. *meine*) in us. With those two conditions, he seems to offer his followers *carte blanche*: "*whatever you ask.*"

Given the millions of prayer requests that have not been fulfilled in the ways the petitioners hoped they would be, we must conclude that either Jesus got it desperately wrong or there is a subtlety that is not immediately apparent in the conditions he mentions. Whatever praying "in Jesus's name" means, it is surely not a magic formula that will guarantee that requests will be granted.

The First Letter of John seems to be saying something closely related to this six-fold promise: "And this is the boldness we have in him, that if we ask anything according to his will, he hears us. And if we know that he hears us in whatever we ask, we know that we have obtained the requests made of him" (1 John 5:14–15).

Jesus said, "Ask anything in my name, and [either] I [or the Father] will do it." His apostle said, "If we ask anything according to his will...we know that we have obtained the requests made of him."

If we assume that—in this instance, at least—asking something "in Jesus's name" is equivalent to asking something "according to the will of God," the question then becomes: how do we know when something is according to the will of God? And the biblical answer seems to be that *God sometimes reveals his will to people in specific situations who then know it by faith.*

Peter Wagner defined it this way: "The gift of faith is the special ability that God gives to certain members of the Body of Christ to discern with extraordinary confidence the will and purposes of God for the future of his work."[54]

The problem for so many people is that a kind of practical fatalism paralyzes their ability to believe and to ask: "If something is God's will, isn't it going to happen anyway? And if it is *not* his will, he isn't going to give it to us—and, in fact, we don't really want it, not ultimately, not with our best self."

This dilemma is exemplified by the agonizing prayer of Jesus himself: "My Father, if it is possible, let this cup pass from me; yet not what I want but what you want" (Matt. 26:39, 42, 44). It was *not* God's will to let that cup pass, Jesus's request was denied, and the inevitable took place. If even *Jesus's three-times-repeated prayer* could not alter the will of God, how could we ever suppose that *ours* will do so?[55]

In encouraging us to ask God for wisdom, James wrote, "But ask in faith, never doubting, for the one who doubts is like a wave of the sea, driven and tossed by the wind; for the doubter, being double-minded and unstable in every way, must not expect to receive anything from the Lord" (James 1:5–8).

If I know with certainty that something is the will of God, why bother to ask? And if I do *not* know, how can I ask without doubting? In the final analysis, the working theology of a great many believers is "whatever will be, will be."

But when we examine some of the great heroes of Scripture, we see a very different pattern. Perhaps the best example is that of Daniel, who wrote, "In the first year of Darius son of Ahasuerus, by birth a Mede, who became king over the realm of the Chaldeans...I, Daniel, perceived in the books the number of years that, according to the

---

54   C. Peter Wagner, *Your Spiritual Gifts* (Ventura: Regal, 2005), 153.

55   It is important to remind ourselves that Jesus qualified his request by saying, "Nevertheless, not my will but yours." In the larger sense of that qualification, his prayer *was* answered in the affirmative.

word of the Lord to the prophet Jeremiah, must be fulfilled for the devastation of Jerusalem, namely, seventy years" (Dan. 9:1–2).

Jeremiah is nicknamed "the weeping prophet" because of the terrible punishment he saw coming upon the people of his day. He predicted—and lived to see his prediction fulfilled—the terrible defeat of Judah by the Babylonians and the ensuing Babylonian captivity.

But twice in his prophecy, he was very explicit that the captivity would be limited to seventy years: "This whole land shall become a ruin and a waste, and these nations shall serve the king of Babylon seventy years. Then after seventy years are completed, I will punish the king of Babylon and that nation, the land of the Chaldeans, for their iniquity, says the Lord, making the land an everlasting waste" (Jer. 25:11–12). And again, "For thus says the Lord: Only when Babylon's seventy years are completed will I visit you, and I will fulfill to you my promise and bring you back to this place" (Jer. 29:10).

Daniel, born in Babylon a generation later, says that he "perceived in the books" (presumably a scroll of Jeremiah's prophecy) that the predicted seventy years had been "fulfilled"—i.e., *it was God's will that his people should now return to their own land.*

And his response to knowing that was to *ask* that they might do so: "O Lord, in view of all your righteous acts, let your anger and wrath, we pray, turn away from your city Jerusalem, your holy mountain; because of our sins and the iniquity of our ancestors, Jerusalem and your people have become a disgrace among all our neighbors. Now therefore, O our God, listen to the prayer of your servant and to his supplication, and for your own sake, Lord, let your face shine upon your desolated sanctuary" (Dan. 9:16–17).

Daniel writes that while he was praying, the "man" Gabriel came to him and said, "Daniel, I have come out to give you wisdom and understanding. At the beginning of your supplications a word went out, and I have come to declare" that the promise of God would indeed be fulfilled because Daniel had asked that it would be (Dan. 9:20).

In this instance, at least, the pattern was not: "God said it; I believe it. That settles it." The pattern was, "God said it; I believe it. Now I will ask according to his will."

Ezekiel was part of the company of Jews carried captive in 598 B.C. by Nebuchadnezzar. Like Jeremiah's prophecy, his prophecy is in large part one of God's severe judgments upon his people. But, suddenly, halfway through the thirty-sixth chapter, there is an abrupt change as God promises to curtail the punishment: "Therefore say to the house of Israel, Thus says the Lord God: It is not for your sake, O house of Israel, that I am about to act, but for the sake of my holy name, which you have profaned among the nations" (Ezek. 36:22).

Through the prophet, God piles up promise after promise of what he will certainly do:

- "I will sanctify my great name...and the nations shall know that I am the Lord" (Ezek. 36:23).

- "I will take you from the nations...and bring you into your own land" (Ezek. 36:24).

- "I will sprinkle clean water upon you, and you shall be clean from all your uncleanness" (Ezek. 36:25).

- "I will cleanse you" (Ezek. 36:25).

- "A new heart I will give you, and a new spirit I will put within you" (Ezek. 36:26).

- "I will remove from your body the heart of stone and give you a heart of flesh" (Ezek. 36:26).

- "I will put my spirit within you" (Ezek. 36:27).

- "Then you shall live in the land that I gave to your ancestors; and you shall be my people, and I will be your God" (Ezek. 36:28).

- "I will save you" (Ezek. 36:29).

- "I will make the fruit of the tree and the produce of the field abundant" (Ezek. 36:30).

- "I will cause the towns to be inhabited, and the waste places shall be rebuilt" (Ezek. 36:33).

- "The land that was desolate shall be tilled, instead of being the desolation that it was in the sight of all who passed by. And they will say, 'This land that was desolate has become like the garden of Eden'" (Ezek. 36:34–35).

- "Then the nations that are left all around you shall know that I, the Lord, have rebuilt the ruined places, and replanted that which was desolate; I, the Lord, have spoken, and I will do it" (Ezek. 36:36).

"I will do this, and I will do this, and I will do this; I have spoken, and I will do it." And where does this crescendo of promises reach its climax? With this final promise: "Thus says the Lord God: *I will also let the house of Israel ask me to do this for them*" (Ezek. 36:37).

"I will do this, and I will do this, and I will do this; and I will also let them *ask me* to do this!" In other words, "*I will do it when they ask me to do it!*" Our agreement with God in prayer might be compared to the second signature on a check or the second key in the safe deposit box. He has stated his will. He waits for us to agree with it.

So, once again, "If we ask anything according to his will, he hears us. And if we know that he hears us in whatever we ask, we know that we have obtained the requests made of him" (1 John 5:14–15). Faith is knowing that God means what he says and he will do what he says. Faith is kindled, or "quickened," by the Word of God written, by words of knowledge and prophecy, and sometimes simply by a sudden, powerful, inner conviction.

TWO HEALINGS IN TANZANIA

In 1981, I was invited to do a teaching series in the Diocese of Western Tanganyika. My wife, Karen, accompanied me. I had not originally planned to speak very much about the healing ministry of the Holy Spirit and the gift of faith to believe him for it. But there was intense interest when I mentioned that we had witnessed some remarkable healings in my parish in Virginia.

There was a good deal of sickness among the people, and doctors were few and medicine was scarce. Additionally, the area had originally been evangelized by British evangelical Anglicans, who taught that the gifts of the Holy Spirit were for the apostolic age and no longer operative. When I said otherwise, there were many who asked for prayer.

Two vignettes are worth recounting.

In midweek, someone said, "If you really believe in the power of prayer, go pray for the Archdeacon." I said, "Archdeacon, what is the trouble?" He opened his mouth and showed me ulcers that went as far down into his throat as I could see, and he said they continued all the way to his stomach. I asked, "Would you like me to pray for you?" He replied, "I don't believe in that stuff!" I said, "I didn't ask if you believed in it; I asked if you would like me to pray for you." He said, "Well, if you have to."

I prayed and saw no immediate result. But he showed up at another meeting on Saturday, when he was supposed to have traveled to the capital, Dar es Salam, for treatment. I said, "Archdeacon, how are you doing?" He opened his mouth again to show me he was completely healed! "But I still don't believe in it!" he added.

Perhaps, but those who had been seeing healings all that week did.

Late on Saturday, one of the priests asked if Karen and I would go with him to his village to pray for his infant daughter. We drove to a clearing where there was a circle of mud huts with thatched roofs. His wife brought the baby, Christine, out and placed her in my arms. I asked, "What is the problem?" "Her tongue is tied, and her womanhood is broken." I prayed for her, and we sang "Jesus Loves Me" as tears rolled down all our faces.

Again, there was no immediate result. But when I returned home, I wrote to the priest: "If we could get Christine to Dar es Salam, both of those problems could be fixed medically. May I send you the money to make that happen?" My letter crossed with his in the mail. He wrote to say that in the few days that followed that visit, God miraculously repaired both problems. We have kept in touch over the years, and Christine is now a mother with children of her own. She never again experienced any problem with either of her original conditions.

I believe God gave the gift of faith to that young priest and his wife, and God honored that faith as they asked "according to his will."

Faith is like a muscle. When we exercise it, it will grow, and we will be more receptive to receiving a gift of faith from the Lord to meet a specific need in a specific situation. The gift of faith is virtually always working in tandem with other gifts of the Holy Spirit whenever and wherever they are operative.

CHAPTER 11

GIFTS OF HEALING

"To another gifts of healing."

—I CORINTHIANS 12:9

OST OF OUR English translations render the next manifestation of the Spirit in St. Paul's list of gifts as "gifts of healing" (1 Cor. 12:9). But in the original, it is a double plural: "gifts of healings (or cures)" (Gk. *charismata iamaton*). This suggests that we will look in vain for a singular pattern or "formula" in the healing miracles of Jesus. Sometimes he leaves what he is doing and goes to the sick (or dying or dead) person (Matt. 9:18–26). Other times he simply speaks a word where he is (Matt. 8:5–13). Sometimes he lays his hands on a person, and in at least in one instance he did so twice, the first time producing only a partial healing (Mark 8:22–26). In a miracle prefiguring his own resurrection, he delayed until a sickness became a death to make the "cure" more significant (John 11:1–44).

Sometimes he heals by casting out a "spirit of infirmity" (Luke 13:11, RSV). Other times he treats an illness or paralysis as a medical problem (Matt. 8:14). Sometimes he pronounces forgiveness before he addresses the physical problem (Matt. 9:2–8). And sometimes, but not always, he commends the faith of the recipient or his or her parents or friends (Luke 17:11–19). Sometimes he is angered by those who seek to accuse him or by the faithlessness of those around him or by the demonic spirit that is causing the problem (Mark 3:5; 9:19, 25). And sometimes he suggests there is a connection between (some) sin and (some) suffering (John 5:14). Other times he says just the opposite (John 9:3).

(There is a wonderful apocryphal story about two men who met in Jerusalem, and as they shared their stories with each other, they discovered they had both been healed of blindness by Jesus. "Tell me how he did it," said one to the other. "He just said, 'Be healed,' and I was healed." "No, no," said the other. "He must spit, make mud, rub it on your eyes, and send you to wash in the pool of Siloam.")

If God (or in this case, if Jesus) has done something one way in the past, our natural tendency is to expect him to do it the same way in the future! But when we examine the gospel record, we see almost endless variation in the healing "methods" Jesus employed.

There are twenty-six healing miracles recounted in various degrees of detail in the four canonical gospels (and there is sometimes a fair amount of disagreement as to those details in the different ways the evangelists tell their stories).[56] These are in addition to a dozen passages that speak of him healing "many" or "all" or "the blind and the lame" or "those who needed to be cured."[57]

---

56 Matthew, Mark, and Luke all tell the story of blind Bartimaeus, for instance (though only Mark names him), but Matthew tells us he was one of *two* blind men healed "as they were leaving Jericho." Mark and Luke tell us only of Bartimaeus, but Luke says it was as Jesus was *approaching* Jericho.

57 Matt. 8:16; 9:35; 14:36; 21:14; Mark 1:32; 3:10; 5:56; Luke 4:40, 41; 5:15; 6:19; 7:21; 9:11

The healing miracles are recounted in the following passages:[58]

Recipients	Matthew	Mark	Luke	John
A leper	8:1–4	1:40–42	5:12–14	
A centurion's slave	8:5–13		7:1–10	
Peter's mother-in-law	8:14	1:30–31	4:38–39	
The Gadarene demoniac(s)	8:28–34	5:1–20	8:26–29	
A paralytic brought by friends	9:2–8	2:3–12	5:17–26	
Jairus's daughter	9:18–26	5:21–43	8:40–56	
A woman with hemorrhages	9:20–22	5:25–34	8:43–48	
Two blind men	9:27–31			
A mute demoniac	9:32–34		11:14–23	
A man with a withered hand	12:9–14	3:1–5	6:6–11	
A blind and mute demoniac	12:22			
A Canaanite daughter	15:21–28	7:24–30		
An (apparently) epileptic boy	17:14–18	9:14–29	9:37–43	
Bartimaeus (and another?)	20:29–34	10:46–52	18:35–43	
A demoniac in a synagogue		1:21–27	4:31–37	
A deaf man with a speech impediment		7:31–37		
A blind man touched twice		8:22–25		
The son of a widow of Nain			7:11–17	
A crippled woman			13:10–17	
A man with dropsy			14:1–6	
Ten lepers			17:11–19	
Malchus's ear			22:51	18:10–11
An official's son				4:46–53
A paralytic at Bethzatha				5:2–15
A man born blind				9:1–41
Lazarus				11:1–44

---

58 These could be presented in any number of formats. I simply followed the chronological order of Matthew, first, and then cross-referenced the other gospels. Then I did the same thing with each of the other three gospels.

Twenty-six healing miracles are recorded in detail, but in only seventeen of them is Jesus *asked* to intervene. Note: how many times did he say yes? *To all of them, plus nine more!* (In addition, remember all the passages that spoke of his healing "many," and "all," and "every disease and sickness.")

Evidently, Jesus was more eager to heal people than they were to ask him to do so.

In eight of these healings, faith is neither mentioned nor demonstrated on anyone's part other than Jesus.[59] Evidently, Jesus was at least sometimes able to heal people when they neither had nor exhibited faith in him to do so.

We remember, of course, that when he visited his hometown, "he could do no deed of power there, except that he laid his hands on a few sick people and cured them. And he was amazed at their unbelief" (Luke 6:5–6). (Most of us would be thrilled with the curing of a few sick people! But Jesus apparently wished he could do more and was somehow hindered by his neighbors' lack of faith.)

The critical issue is that he healed, just as God does in every healing that ever takes place. He desired that sick people get well.

There is clearly a tension and a mystery here, but if Jesus demonstrates to us the desire and will of his Father ("Whoever has seen me has seen the Father" [John 14:8]), it becomes very difficult to conclude that God is ambivalent regarding our health.

The apostle John wrote to his friend Gaius, "Beloved, I pray that all may go well with you and that you may be in good health, just as it is well with your soul" (3 John 2). If we do not begin with the assumption that God desires our good health and that of others, why would we dare go to a doctor? Doing so might be in opposition to the will of God!

(It might be good to remind ourselves that the best doctors will say that they are only instruments in the hands of the Great Physician; it is God who effects the healing.)

---

59 I include among those who had "faith" even the demoniacs who protested, in that they clearly understood Jesus had the authority to do with them as he wished.

He wills our wholeness, but his will can be hindered by doubt and unbelief, by a refusal or inability to receive what he wants to give, by persistence in disobedience and the refusal to repent, by unconfessed sin, by broken relationships and discord in the body of Christ, by self-neglect or abuse, or by the sins of one generation being visited upon another.

He wills your health and mine, but if we smoke three packs of cigarettes a day…or drink a quart of whisky each night…or allow ourselves to be eaten up by pride, jealousy, anger, or bitterness…or are promiscuous and flout his instructions regarding sexual purity…or abuse our children…or refuse to ask for healing prayer from those available to pray for the sick, his will for our well-being may not be realized.

His disciples asked Jesus about the man born blind: "Rabbi, who sinned, this man or his parents, that he was born blind?" Jesus answered, "Neither this man nor his parents sinned; he was born blind so that God's works might be revealed in him" (John 9:2–3).

Illness-in-general is a consequence of sin-in-general; that is, it is all the product of the fall. But usually we cannot draw a one-for-one relationship between a specific illness and a specific sin. We cannot say that because a given person has not (yet) been healed, it is necessarily the result of sin, or unbelief, or any of the other possible factors. The world is simply too complex to reduce things to a formula.

What we can say is that whenever God allows illness or injury to come into a person's life, it is so his own glory might be made manifest in that situation. Sometimes that happens (as in the story of the man born blind) by the person being healed. And sometimes it happens by the sufficiency of God's grace to enable the person to cope.

Paul wrote to the Philippians, "I have learned to be content with whatever I have. I know what it is to have little, and I know what it is to have plenty. In any and all circumstances I have learned the secret of being well-fed and of going hungry. I can do all things in him who strengthens me" (Phil. 4:11–13).

To the Corinthians, Paul wrote: "To keep me from being too elated, a thorn was given me in the flesh, a messenger from Satan to torment me, to keep me from being too elated. Three times I appealed to the Lord about this, that it would leave me, but he said to me, 'My grace is sufficient for you, for power is made perfect in weakness.' So, I will boast all the more gladly of my weaknesses, so that the power of Christ may dwell in me" (2 Cor. 12:7–9).[60]

Earlier Paul had made this promise: "No testing [trial or temptation] has overtaken you that is not common to everyone. God is faithful, and he will not let you be tested [tried, tempted] beyond your strength, but with the testing [trial, temptation] he will also provide the way out so that you may be able to endure it" (1 Cor. 10:13).

James wrote in his letter, "Are any among you sick? They should call for the elders of the church and have them pray over them, anointing them with oil in the name of the Lord. The prayer of faith will save the sick, and the Lord will raise them up; and anyone who has committed sins will be forgiven" (James 5:14–15).

If it is the "prayer of faith" that saves the sick, how much is that prayer undercut by adding to it the phrase "if it be your will"? The ministry of healing begins with the confidence that God desires that healing, even though there may be things that hinder it.

Perhaps the most startling thing about the healing ministry of Jesus is that there is not a single recorded instance of his asking God to heal someone. Jesus commanded healing, and people were healed.

We do know his pattern was to rise early in the morning to pray, and sometimes to spend the whole night in prayer, and no doubt that involved both his seeking the direction and guidance of his Father and readying himself for whatever the day would hold.

While we know God's desire is always the well-being and health of a person, and while it is always right to pray for God to heal, we do not always know the conditions involved that mitigate against healing. And we do not always have the gift of faith in a specific situation to command healing.

---

60 Many commentators question whether this "thorn" was a physical ailment, suggesting instead that it may have been the Judaizers or the "super apostles" who were attacking Paul's ministry. The principle would seem to be the same either way: "I asked that the problem be removed, but God said 'I will give you the grace to cope with it, instead.'"

A "Command Performance"

During the first five years of my ordained ministry, I was a chaplain in two different preparatory high schools in Connecticut. We participated in the Fellowship of Christians in Universities and Schools (FOCUS) that took students and adults to New Hampshire during Christmas break to ski during the day and then gather around a fire in the evening to talk about what it means to be a follower of Christ.

On New Year's Eve one year, we had freezing rain over snow all day, and the mountain was sheer ice. The weather finally lifted, and some of the students went out to sled and toboggan. Suddenly one of the girls sledded right into a tree, bashing her head very badly. She immediately went into convulsions, with tears and screaming.

We got her into the building, where she continued writhing in pain. And the question was: what can we possibly do? The nearest hospital was forty minutes away under the best of conditions; this was New Year's Eve, and the roads were glare ice.

We said, "Let's pray." And I heard coming out of my mouth something I had never said before. Instead of, "Oh God, please heal her," I said, "In the name of Jesus, be healed!"

Her tears and convulsions stopped immediately, and a huge smile replaced them as she said, "Oh, I'm going to know him now!" "You mean you didn't?" I said. "No, but I am going to know him now."

And she did, and she does.

CHAPTER 12

MIRACLES

"To another the working of miracles."

—1 CORINTHIANS 12:10

ONCE AGAIN, IN the original text, the phrase "the working of miracles" (or "miraculous powers," NIV) is actually a double plural, literally "operations of powers" (Gk. *energemata dunameon*). But where we saw no single pattern in the healing miracles of Jesus, there is a rather startling dimension to the other ten miracles recorded in the gospels, all of which pertain to the interruption of nature.

They are not *fantastic* like the things that happen in Grimm's fairy tales. They are not like kissing frogs that then turn into princes. They are, in large measure, *replications on a different scale and at a different speed of what God has been doing in the past or what he promises to do in the future.*[61]

---

61 I am indebted for this insight to C. S. Lewis, who developed it in a somewhat similar way in his *Miracles: A Preliminary Study* (New York: Macmillan, 1947); see especially p. 142.

The other miracles of Jesus are recounted in the following passages:

Event	Matthew	Mark	Luke	John
Changing water to wine				2:1–11
First catch of fish			5:1–11	
Stilling the sea	8:23–27	4:35–41	8:22–25	
Feeding 5,000 (+?)	14:13–21	6:32–44	9:10–17	
Walking on water	14:22–33	6:45–51		
Feeding 4,000	15:32–39	8:1–10		
Money in a fish's mouth	17:24–27			
Withering a fig tree	21:18–22	11:12–24		
Appearing in locked room				20:19–23
Second catch of fish				21:1–14

Let us consider some illustrations.

Every year, God sends rain to water the earth. Plants of all kinds send their roots deep into the ground to drink up that life-giving moisture. If conditions of temperature and sunshine are right, at the end of the growing season, farmers and vine growers go into their fields to harvest the corn, wheat, barley, and other vegetables and grapes and other fruit.

The vine growers will crush their grapes to make a lovely, drinkable juice. (If they are Baptists, they will stop right there! But if they have the good sense to be Episcopalians, they will put the best juices into kegs that are stored in a cool cellar for months or years.) And finally, when the time is right, they will tap those kegs, and the juice, now fermented, will have become wine. Water has become wine!

But it happened so slowly that some people might not have thought it a miracle: "That's just the way it is." Or they might have attributed it to the wrong "person": Mother Nature, Bacchus, or Dionysus.

But when the Son of God stepped onto the stage of human history, he did the same thing in an instant, and suddenly the mask was off: this is not the work of Mother Nature or any pagan deity; this is the work of the God of history (John 2:1–11).

The farmers gather in their corn and other grains. And then they have a choice to make. They could grind that grain into flour and make a small batch of bread, or they might save that grain for a year or more and use it to plant their fields for a far larger harvest. In effect, they could turn what would have made a small amount of bread into enough to feed a multitude.

Again, it happens so slowly that some might miss the miracle or attribute it to Ceres, or Adonis, or the Corn King. But when the Son of God took a small amount of bread and fed a multitude with it, the mask came off: this was not Ceres, Adonis, or the Corn King; this was the work of the God who provides food for his people year after year (Matt. 14:13–21).[62]

Every year, two fish get together, and from their spawning a whole school of fish is produced, once again, enough to feed a multitude. To some it might not seem a miracle. But when the Son of God multiplied two fish to feed a multitude, there surely was an echo of God's promise to Noah that all the fish of the sea would be delivered into his hand.[63]

When Jesus rebuked the storm and calmed the sea, we might wonder whether his disciples remembered the words of Psalm 107: "Then they cried to the Lord in their trouble, and he brought them out from their distress; he made the storm still, and the waves of the sea were hushed."[64] He had authority even over nature.

When Jesus walked on water, did any of his disciples recall God's taunting question of Job: "Have you entered into the springs of the sea, or walked in the recesses of the deep?"[65] What God could do, Jesus could do!

When Jesus instructed Peter to catch a fish because he would find in its mouth a coin (Gk. *statera*) to pay the temple tax, did Peter reflect on the fact that when God instructed his ancient people to build the temple itself, he said, "The silver is mine, and the gold is mine, says

---

62 This is usually called "the feeding of the five thousand," but Matthew says there were "about five thousand *men*, besides women and children."

63 Mark 6:32–44; cf. Genesis 9:2

64 Psalm 107:28–29; cf. Mark 4:35–41

65 Job 38:16; cf. Matthew 14:22–33

the Lord of hosts"?[66] Note: it might be debated as to whether this was a miracle of *creation*—i.e., that Jesus somehow *caused* the coin to be there—or another instance of Jesus speaking a (most unusual) "word of knowledge" that it would be there.

When Jesus cursed the fig tree and it withered abruptly, did anyone compare it to God sending the plague of locusts that left "nothing green...no tree, no plant in the field, in all the land of Egypt"?[67]

And when Jesus appeared in the midst of his disciples in a locked room on Easter evening, it surely foreshadowed a time he himself predicted: "in the resurrection [we will be] like angels in heaven."[68]

When Jesus healed the paralytic at the pool of Bethzatha, the Jews accused him of breaking the Sabbath (by telling the man to carry his mat). Jesus's response was, "My Father is still working, and I also am working" (John 5:17). He was making two extraordinary statements at the same time. First, he was asserting that the common Jewish view of the Sabbath was a complete misunderstanding of its purpose and, behind it, a misunderstanding of the character of God.

(On another occasion, Jesus said, "The Sabbath was made for humankind, and not humankind for the Sabbath" (Mark 2:27). In other words, it was a *gift* from God that we should have a day off from work each week, not an inflexible rule that prevents the doing of good. It was an expression of God's love for us that he would give such a gift. In effect, he said, "You have totally mischaracterized both the Sabbath itself and God's purpose in giving it. My Father *delights* to heal people on the Sabbath.")

And secondly, he was saying, "God is my Father," my Daddy, my *Abba*. In the Hebrew Scriptures, God is sometimes spoken of as the "Father" of the nation (Isa. 63:16), and he calls himself the "Father" of David (Ps. 89:26), and the "Father" of orphans and the protector of widows (Ps. 68:5). But no good Jew of Jesus's time would dare to call God "my Father." It would be considered blasphemy. And, indeed, in

---

66   Haggai 2:8; cf. Matthew 17:24–27

67   Exodus 10:15; cf. Matthew 21:18–22

68   Matthew 22:30; cf. John 20:19–23

the story of this healing, that is exactly how the Jews took it. We read, "For this reason the Jews were seeking all the more to kill him, because he was not only breaking the Sabbath, but was also calling God his own Father, thereby making himself equal with God" (John 5:18).

This, of course, is the very central point in the claims of Christ. Is he, indeed, God come among us, the "Word" and very Son of God? Or is he a madman or perhaps the worst blasphemer the world has ever known? Jesus's answer to his accusers was one of the most important keys to his life and ministry: "Very truly, I tell you, the Son can do nothing on his own, but only what he sees the Father doing; for whatever the Father does, the Son does likewise" (John 5:19).

This, in its immediate context, was Jesus's justification and explanation for the healing of the paralytic. Somehow he discerned that the Father was eager to heal this particular man of his nearly four decades of paralysis. The story tells us that a multitude of invalids were gathered at the pool that day.[69] But we are told of no other healings than this one. Jesus discerned that his Father was eager to heal this man, and perhaps the man was ready to believe, and Jesus joined his Father in causing it to occur.[70]

We get the sense, in reading the Gospels, that Jesus was very open to a new word from his Father, or a fresh prompting from the Spirit. It is the only way we can understand his abrupt reversals of himself.

---

69   The legend was that from time to time an angel of the Lord would come to the pool and stir the water. No one could see the angel, but they would know he was there because of the way the water was suddenly troubled. And the first one into the pool would receive healing. Whether there was any factual basis for this legend, we have no way of knowing. But wherever there have been reports of supernatural healing, others will gather, hoping to be the next ones to receive similar healings. At the Shrine of Our Lady of Lourdes in France, the Roman Catholic Church has officially recognized sixty-seven miraculous healings. And since 1860, it is estimated that more than 200 million visitors have made pilgrimages to the shrine, many of them hoping for healings.

70   The man first expressed his belief that he needed to get into the pool, but when Jesus told him to "stand up, take your mat and walk," he took the risk of doing so. Legs that had been paralyzed for thirty-eight years would have been brittle. His muscles would have atrophied, his joints calcified. That he rolled over and risked having his legs collapse beneath him, leaving him in a far worse condition than beforehand would seem to be an expression of *his* faith that somehow Jesus had the power and authority to effect this healing.

His mother asks him to rescue a wedding party that has run out of wine, and his response sounds almost like a rebuff: "Woman, what concern is that to you and to me? My hour has not yet come" (John 2:4). Two verses later, we see Jesus saving the party with the miraculous changing of water into the best wine of the day (John 2:7–11). What happened? Clearly, there were fresh instructions from the Father. ("My hour has not yet come...Oh! I guess it has!")

Jesus's brothers urge him to go to Jerusalem for the Feast of Booths, and once again he says, "My hour has not yet come...I am not going to this festival" (John 7:6, 8). And once again, just two verses later, he goes to the Festival. Was he lying to his brothers? Much more likely, he had new instructions from his Father.

But in a larger sense, Jesus's response to his accusers at the pool of Bethzatha was a kind of grid for examining all of his miracles. They were in perfect harmony with "whatever the Father does." Not *fantastic*, just *wonderful*.

In the story of the healing of the man blind from birth, John tells us of Jesus spitting, making mud, and spreading the mud on the man's eyes, then telling him to go wash in the pool of Siloam.[71] When the man returned, now able to see, his neighbors argued as to whether or not it was the same man. Some said it was, and others said it was someone "like" him.

It is *possible* that Jesus chose this strange method for healing this particular man because his eyes were damaged or even missing, and that rather than *healing* him in the ordinary sense of the word, Jesus was actually *creating* eyes out of the mud, replicating the creation of Adam from the dust of the ground. Perhaps he looked different to his neighbors because of the change in the appearance of his eyes.

In any event, in all these ways, Jesus *replicated* what his Father has been doing, year after year, season after season—or in some cases, he *foreshadowed* what God promises to do in the future. The raising of Lazarus, for instance, prefigures our resurrection on the last day.

---

71 The story is recounted in great detail in John 9, just about in the middle of John's gospel. John obviously considered it a miracle of great significance.

Jesus's ministry was one of signs and wonders, and it was under the anointing of the Holy Spirit. When Peter explained the gospel to the centurion, Cornelius, and his household, he put it this way:

> The message spread throughout Judea, beginning in Galilee after the baptism that John announced: how God anointed Jesus of Nazareth with the Holy Spirit and with power; how he went about doing good and healing all who were oppressed by the devil, for God was with him.
>
> —ACTS 10:37–38

CHAPTER 13

GREATER WORKS THAN THESE (A PARENTHETICAL COMMENT)

"Very truly, I tell you, the one who believes in me will
also do the works that I do and, in fact, will do greater
works than these, because I am going to the Father."

—JOHN 14:12

TAKEN AT FACE value, Jesus's statement seems to imply that his followers are either going to do even more *spectacular* miracles than he did or they are going to do *numerically more* of them (or both). While there have been claims that every one of Jesus's miracles has been replicated at various points in Christian history,[72] any honest assessment will have to admit they have never been more abundant or more spectacular than his.

There may have been great "signs and wonders" associated with Christian ministry from time to time, but no one has ever claimed to have performed more miracles, or more dramatic miracles, than Jesus himself.

---

72 The British evangelist Smith Wigglesworth (1859–1947) claimed to have raised as many as thirty-three people from the dead, including his wife, Polly. See Wikipedia. org, "Smith Wigglesworth," http://en.wikipedia.org/wiki/Smith_Wigglesworth. See also Stanley Howard Frodsham, *Smith Wigglesworth: Apostle of Faith* (Springfield: Gospel Publishing House, 1972). More recently, claims of the dead being raised have been attributed to the ministry of Reinhard Bonnke (1940–). See Aaron Rogers, "Reinhard Bonnke," *Supernatural Signs and Wonders* (blog), January 20, 2009, http://www.supernaturalsigns .com/2009/01/20/reinhard-bonnke/.

But just as we saw in earlier chapters, there may be a subtlety in this promise that is not immediately apparent. Early in Jesus's ministry, he asked his disciples, "Who do people say that the Son of Man is?" (Matt. 16:13). They gave him a variety of answers. But then he pressed the question: "Who do you say that I am?" (Matt. 16:15). Peter, speaking for all the disciples, responded, "You are the Messiah, the Son of the living God" (Matt. 16:16). Jesus commended this answer and said it had been revealed to Peter by "my Father in heaven" (Matt. 16:17).

Matthew records that "*from that time on*, Jesus began to show his disciples that he must go to Jerusalem and undergo great suffering at the hands of the elders and chief priests and scribes, and be killed, and on the third day be raised" (Matt. 16:21).

From the first time someone recognized Jesus as the Messiah and the Son of God (however little he understood what that meant), Jesus began to teach that his ultimate purpose was to suffer, die, and be raised from the dead. However often he returned to the subject, his disciples either could not or would not accept his teaching.[73] But he was very clear that out of all the things he came to do: "bring good news to the poor...proclaim release to the captives and recovery of sight to the blind... let the oppressed go free, [and] proclaim the year of the Lord's favor" (Luke 4:18–19), to "show us the Father" (John 14:8), "to destroy the works of the devil" (1 John 3:8), his central-most purpose was "to give his life a ransom for many" (Matt. 20:28).This leads to a very strangely paradoxical conclusion: *as truly astonishing as Jesus's earthly ministry obviously was, prior to his crucifixion, death, and resurrection, that ministry was incomplete.*

If the good news of the Christian gospel is that Jesus has finally and completely set us free by dying on a cross for our sins, descending into hell for three days, rising from the grave, and ascending to the Father, then *prior* to all of that actually happening, *Jesus's own message was not fully Christian!*

He himself was the message, but the message was not complete until he accomplished what he came to do. This is why he said to his

---

73   Cf. Mark 9:32; Luke 9:45; 18:34

disciples, "I still have many things to say to you, but you cannot bear them now. When the Spirit of truth comes, he will guide you into all the truth; for he will not speak on his own, but will speak whatever he hears, and he will declare to you the things that are to come. He will glorify me, because he will take what is mine and declare it to you" (John 16:12–14).

Even Jesus's miracles were incomplete and temporary. The people he healed all eventually died. Even those whom he raised from the dead all eventually died again.

But the person to whom we explain the gospel, the person who receives it gladly and puts his or her trust in this Lord Jesus, the person who receives new life from God, Jesus said, "will never die" (John 11:26). Their *bodies* will die, but they will live forever (John 3:16).

Rodney Whitacre wrote:

> Earlier Jesus had said it is a blessing for him to return to the Father (John 14:28). Now he adds that it is also for their good that he is going away, for then he will send the Paraclete (John 16:7). The Spirit is already present…but Jesus cannot send the Spirit in his role as Paraclete until he himself has returned to the Father. Why is this? Earlier John had explained that the Spirit was not yet given because Jesus "had not yet been glorified" (John 7:39). Jesus' glorification is his death, resurrection and ascension to the Father, and these provide both the climax of his revelation and a testimony to the truth of his life and teaching. The role of the Spirit is to interpret and bear witness to Jesus and his revelation of the Father (John 16:12–15). So until Jesus has completed his revelation, the Spirit is not able to do his job, for he does not have the full revelation to work with.[74]

Whether it is through an evangelist proclaiming the gospel or a simple Christian witnessing to a friend, if saving faith is born in the hearer, it is a "greater work" than any of the miracles performed by Jesus prior to his death!

---

74   Rodney A. Whitacre, *John*, in the *IVP New Testament Commentary Series* (Downers Grove: InterVarsity Press, 1999), 388–389.

CHAPTER 14

PROPHECY

"To another prophecy."

—I CORINTHIANS 12:10

JESUS WAS NOT only *a* prophet, he was *the* prophet.

The Book of Deuteronomy ends with a paragraph praising Moses: "Never since has there arisen a prophet in Israel like Moses, whom the Lord knew face to face. He was unequaled for all the signs and wonders that the Lord sent him to perform in the land of Egypt, against Pharaoh and all his servants and his entire land, and for all the mighty deeds and all the terrifying displays of power that Moses performed in the sight of all Israel" (Deut. 34:10–12).

Yet earlier in the book, Moses himself had promised, "The Lord your God will raise up for you a prophet like me from among your own people; you shall heed such a prophet" (Deut. 18:15). Moses went on to recount what the Lord had said to him: "They are right in what they have said. I will raise up for them a prophet like you from among their own people; I will put my words in the mouth of the prophet, who shall speak to them everything that I command" (Deut. 18:18).

There were many prophets in the eight and a half centuries between Moses and Malachi, and some of them did impressive signs and wonders. But none of them was recognized as "the prophet like Moses."

Following Malachi, there were four centuries of "silence." There was no word or vision from the Lord to the people whose very existence as a nation was predicated on the fact that the living God directed them, spoke to them, and had chosen them as his own.

No word from God, no prophecy, until John the Baptizer. At the outset of his ministry, a deputation of priests and Levites from Jerusalem questioned him: "Who are you?" (John 1:19). Gail O'Day writes:

> The issue of John's identity must be resolved before the central question of the Gospel, Jesus' identity, can be addressed. The formal, emphatic beginning of v. 20 ("He confessed and did not deny it, but confessed") communicates the solemnity of John's response. John confesses, "I am not the Christ," even though he was not asked whether he was the Messiah. The Greek of John's denial (*ego opuk eimi*, "I am not") provides a pointed contrast with the language Jesus uses to speak about his identity in John (*ego eimi* "I am"). The rhetoric of John's denial thus reinforces its content; he is not the Christ.[75]

The deputation asked John, "What then? Are you Elijah?" He said, "I am not." "Are you *the prophet?*" He answered, "No" (John 1:21). O'Day continues:

> Elijah and the prophet were both figures upon whom some of the messianic expectations of Judaism came to rest. Elijah was transported into heaven without dying (2 Kings 2:11), and many Jews expected his return as the harbinger of the messianic age (e.g., Malachi 4:5). "The prophet" derives from the prophet-like-Moses of Deuteronomy 18:15. In the Qumran community, this prophet was seen as a messianic figure, and similar expectations may lie behind the delegation's question.[76]

As the gospel story unfolds, we find Jesus saying of John, "If you are willing to accept it, he is Elijah who is to come" (Matt. 11:14). He clearly meant this in a figurative sense, i.e., "John is an Elijah-like type," for later in the narrative, on the Mount of Transfiguration,

---

75 Gail R. O'Day, "Commentary on John," in *The New Interpreter's Bible*, vol. 9 (Nashville: Abingdon, 1995), 527.

76 O'Day, "Commentary on John," 527–528.

Jesus has a remarkable interchange with both Moses and Elijah concerning Jesus's "departure" (literally, his *exodus*), that is, his death.[77]

But although they nowhere explicitly say so, it is clear the evangelists (and especially Luke) understood Jesus himself to be "the prophet like Moses" whose ministry was characterized by mighty signs and wonders and "terrifying displays of power."

B. D. Napier wrote:

> If, now, we recall the statement...that "he who is now called a prophet was formerly called a seer," we are justified...in concluding that prophet and seer, by either designation, were understood as exercising in common the function of "seeing"— i.e., apprehending that which is not normally accessible, and "speaking forth," proclaiming, that which is thus seen and apprehended.[78]

It is commonly said that "prophecy included (or includes) *foretelling*, but it is primarily *forthtelling*," that is, speaking God's word into a given situation, pronouncing his judgment on people and events. Generally speaking, there were/are two kinds of prophecy: prophecies or oracles of blessing (or "weal"), and prophecies or oracles of judgment (or "woe").

The most dramatic instance of Jesus pronouncing both kinds of oracles is in what some have called "the sermon on the plain" (in contrast to Matthew's "sermon on the mount"), what Luke calls "a level place."[79] Let us consider the passage. (But recall the point: this was

---

77 Moses was the great lawgiver, and Elijah was the greatest of the pre-exilic prophets. Jesus was, literally, surrounded by the law and the prophets. Peter, as always, eager to get it right, gets it wrong. It was not that Jesus had somehow attained the status of Moses and Elijah; it was that *they* were there to worship *him*. And, no doubt, to encourage him. Moses was buried by God, and Elijah was one of only two men in the Bible who never died (the other being Enoch). In two quite different ways, they knew what it was to "depart" this life, and they were thus able to share with Jesus something that none of his disciples could share.

78 B. D. Napier, "Prophet, Prophetism," in *The Interpreter's Dictionary of the Bible* (Nashville: Abingdon, 1962), 897.

79 There is a great debate as to whether Matthew and Luke are recounting the *same* sermon—the same bit of Jesus's preaching to the disciples and the crowds—or *two quite different moments* in his ministry. If it was the same sermon, there are questions as to how

prophecy, and Jesus was prophesying under the anointing of the Holy Spirit. He was exercising the gift of prophecy.)

> [Jesus] looked up at his disciples and said:
> "Blessed are you who are poor, for yours is the kingdom of God. Blessed are you who are hungry now, for you will be filled. Blessed are you who weep now, for you will laugh. Blessed are you when people hate you, and when they exclude you, revile you, and defame you on account of the Son of Man. Rejoice in that day and leap for joy, for surely your reward is great in heaven; for that is what their ancestors did to the prophets. But woe to you who are rich, for you have received your consolation. Woe to you who are full now, for you will be hungry. Woe to you who are laughing now, for you will mourn and weep. Woe to you when all speak well of you, for that is what their ancestors did to the false prophets."
>
> —LUKE 6:20–26

Matthew's version of "the Beatitudes" is better known, even though it is a good deal longer than Luke's. Luke's is pithier, and although there are fewer statements of God's blessing, they are balanced by statements of his judgment. Matthew has nine beatitudes while Luke has only four. Matthew's version speaks of *inner attitudes* to be cultivated ("Blessed are the poor *in spirit*," "Blessed are those who hunger and thirst *for righteousness*"), whereas Luke speaks of *external conditions* ("Blessed are the *poor*," "Blessed are the *hungry*").

Matthew's are *general* ("Blessed are *the* poor in spirit); Luke's are *personal* ("Blessed are *you* who are poor"). Matthew's beatitudes stand on their own—nine states or conditions of God's blessing attending these inner attitudes that Jesus is commending. But Luke's four pronouncements of God's blessing are balanced by four pronouncements of God's judgment, "woe," for those living in opposite circumstances.

In Matthew's version, Jesus seems to be saying that the right

---

we might understand the obvious differences between the two accounts. And if these were two different sermons, we might wrestle with the question of how they interact with each other. These questions are beyond the scope of this study. For our purposes, we will simply note some of the differences between the two accounts.

attitude—an attitude of meekness, humility, and the desire to be right with God—will lead to his blessing. In Luke, it *sounds as if* Jesus is saying there is blessedness in the circumstances themselves: a blessing in poverty, hunger, weeping, and being ridiculed. And the corollary is that there is a snare, at least, perhaps a curse, in enjoying wealth, satisfaction, merriment, and a good reputation.

When we read Scripture in the light of other Scripture, that is a very difficult position to maintain. Jesus said his own ministry included preaching good news to the poor (Matt. 11:5). He fed the hungry.[80] He said he came to "bind up the brokenhearted."[81] As we have seen, he comforted the bereaved and even restored their loved ones.[82]

Further, when we read these words in the light of human experience, they simply cannot mean what they might seem to.

A VISIT TO INDIA

Several years ago, Karen and I spent a few days in the city of Bombay (now called Mumbai), India. We rode through the streets, and in every direction, as far as we could see, there were people—thousands of them—in abject poverty. The fortunate ones had a piece of cardboard for shelter; most slept on the ground without even that. There was no heat, no running water, no electricity. Early each morning, flatbed trucks moved through the city to pick up the bodies of those who had died during the night. At every intersection, women came up to our car and pounded on our windows, holding up their children who in most cases were maimed or injured in some way, asking us for money—or for us to take the children.

The people we were staying with told us that in most cases, the mothers had inflicted the injuries deliberately, hoping to play on the sympathies of visitors. There are no words that can adequately convey

---

80   Matthew 14:13–21; 15:32–39

81   Luke does not quote that part of Isaiah 61, but he tells Jesus read from the scroll of Isaiah (see Luke 4:17), and he would have read that phrase as part of the passage.

82   Matthew 15:21–28; Luke 7:11–17; John 4:46–53; 11:1–44

the horrors of what we saw. I have absolutely no hesitation in saying: *there is no blessedness in poverty, per se.*

❧

Anyone who has stood at the bedside of a friend in the final stages of cancer or AIDS knows *there is no blessedness in illness, per se.*

Those who have visited Haiti since the earthquake in early 2011 know *there is no blessedness in hunger, per se.*

Janani Luwum was Archbishop of Uganda until Idi Amin arrested him, tortured him, castrated him, and murdered him. I know that he personally did it because my friend, Bishop Festo Kivengere, of Kigezi, was there and told me about it. *There is no blessing in being tortured, per se.*

Jesus told a parable about a certain rich man who went to hell (Luke 16:19–31)—not *because* he was rich, but because in the midst of his riches, he lived for himself, not for God, not for others. Outside his door, there was a beggar named Lazarus who also died. He went to Abraham's bosom—not *because* he had nothing in this life but because in the midst of his poverty, he put his trust in God.

Read the parable superficially and it might look like it is a matter of a simple reversal of fortunes, i.e., you have comfort now? Enjoy it, because you will not have it in the hereafter. You do not have comfort now? Not to worry; there is "pie in the sky when you die, bye and bye."

That is not even vaguely Jesus's point! His concern is the "great chasm" between heaven and hell. The rich man calls to Father Abraham, asking him to send Lazarus to warn his brothers against living for themselves and going to hell. Abraham replies, "If they will not listen to Moses and the prophets, neither will they be convinced even if someone should rise from the dead" (Luke 16:31).

Neither Jesus himself, nor scripture generally, ever suggests that wealth in and of itself is inherently sinful. Wealth is like bricks. We can use bricks to build a cathedral, or we can use them to bash our neighbor over the head. The bricks themselves are neutral. It is what we do with them that matters. And so it is with money.

Jesus told the rich young man to sell what he had and give it to the poor (Mark 10:17–22)[83]—because he had made a god of his money, and it prevented him following the true God and giving him first place in his life. He had become possessed by his possessions.

This is the context in which we must hear Jesus's oracles of blessing and judgment. He is not saying that terrible circumstances are a blessing from God. He is saying *there is a blessing to be found in inviting God into our sometimes terrible circumstances.* He is not saying there is judgment from God upon all creature comforts. He is saying *there is great danger in living for creature comforts and missing God.*

But the point is: He was *prophesying.*

FINDING THE BLESSING IN
DIFFICULT CIRCUMSTANCES

When I was in seminary, my field work was working with college students in New England for InterVarsity Christian Fellowship. My regional director told me to go visit a woman named Addie Woram who lived in the Jerome Nursing Home in New Britain, Connecticut. She was, he said, "a prayer warrior," and she would pray for me. (I did not know exactly what a "prayer warrior" was, and I was not at all sure I wanted to meet one! But I went.)

I found Mrs. Woram in a small, darkened bedroom. She kept the

---

83   The man called Jesus "Good Teacher," and Jesus responded by asking him, "Why do you call me good? No one is good but God alone." Far from being a denial of his divinity, this turns out to be a remarkably strong, though indirect, claim to it. When Jesus quoted the commandments, He mentioned only the latter six, and He changed the tenth from "Do not covet" to "You shall not defraud." The man had the temerity to say, "I have kept all these from my youth." Rather than calling him a liar, Jesus "loved him" and said, "You lack one thing." If he had kept the latter six commandments—which deal with our horizontal relationships with our neighbors—but he still lacked one thing, it could only be his relationship to God, as expressed in the first four commandments. Jesus summed up the whole of that responsibility in two words: "Follow me." Jesus changed the tenth commandment because this man's problem was precisely that he coveted. Matthew, Mark, and Luke all recount this story, with intriguingly different details. Mark has Jesus changing the tenth commandment into "Do not defraud" (10:19). Matthew has him substituting the "second great commandment" for it: "You shall love your neighbor as yourself" (19:19). And Luke leaves it out altogether. The changes would certainly have been noticed by the man himself as Jesus subtly and gently exposed his problem.

lights low because brightness bothered her eyes. She wore plastic gloves because she had severe psoriasis, and she was bent over with arthritis. As we made our introductions, she told me that her husband had died twenty years earlier, and her only son ten years earlier. She also told me that bedroom was her world. The nursing home gave her an allowance of ten dollars a month.

And she was absolutely radiant!

I stammered, "Mrs. Woram, forgive me for asking, but how can you be so joyful?" I shall never forget her answer: "*When you have lost everything else, you discover that Jesus is sufficient.*"

Yes, she would pray for me, and in addition she would tithe her ten dollars to support my ministry.

Even back then, it cost more than a dollar to process a gift. So her tithe was literally worthless. And it was the most valuable gift I have ever received. If I may borrow the words of Jesus, "Whenever this good news is proclaimed in the whole world, what she has done will be told in remembrance of her" (Matt. 26:13).

"The Little Apocalypse" recorded in Matthew 24 and 25, Mark 13, and Luke 21 is the most extended example of Jesus's predictive prophecy. More broadly, he claimed that *everything* he said was from God: "The words that I say to you I do not speak on my own; but the Father who dwells in me does his works" (John 14:10).

Jesus was, among all the other things, a prophet. He was, in fact, "*the* prophet," and more—he was, and is, the very Word of God. He himself was Prophecy incarnate. A very great deal of his preaching was prophecy. And he prophesied under the anointing of the Holy Spirit, for he said "[the Holy Spirit] has anointed me to preach" (Luke 4:18, rsv).

In the Church

At the center of his discussion of the gifts of the Spirit, St. Paul has a double exhortation: "Strive for the greater gifts…Pursue love and strive for the spiritual gifts, and *especially that you may prophesy*" (1 Cor. 12:32; 14:1). He goes on to make the remarkable comment that "you can all prophesy one by one, so that all may learn and be encouraged" (1 Cor. 14:31).

Sinclair Ferguson comments:

> Recently a number of writers have suggested that in the New Testament we encounter two levels of prophetic ministry: (1) that associated with the apostles and characterized by an implicit claim to infallibility, and (2) a second level of prophecy which lays claim to divinely-given insight, but not necessarily to infallibility of utterance.[84]

This would certainly seem to be the case in those churches which encourage sharing the gifts of the Spirit in worship. Usually "prophecy" is expressed as a word of encouragement, and sometimes direction or even warning or rebuke, but not on the level of the authority of Scripture, e.g.: "The Lord would say to you, 'I know that some of you are deeply worried and frightened tonight. Do not be afraid; I am with you. I know the plans I have for you, and they are plans for your welfare. Trust me, for my love for you will never fail.'"

"Prophecy" of this sort seems to be a matter of "hearing" or "sensing" that God has a message for the people gathered and giving voice to that message.

George Malone wrote:

> As the character of one giving prophecy is to be examined within the context of the community, so prophecy, given in the context of worship, is to be judged (1 Corinthians 14:29). Those who make the judgment are most likely fellow prophets and overseers of the church (1 Thessalonians 5:12–22). Although a person's motives may be pure and he may have a "feeling of inspiration," there are no guarantees that the Lord indeed is speaking. So the apostles were continually reminding the

---

84 Ferguson, *The Holy Spirit*, 214.

churches to examine the source of the communication (1 John 4:1, 1 Thessalonians 5:21).[85]

James Dunn added:

> The more highly valued a word of prophecy is by the church, the more open is that church to deception, the more liable it is to be led astray by false prophecy. Failure to recognize the role of discerning of spirits means failure to recognize the character of prophecy and prevents the gift of prophecy functioning properly. As in the worshipping assembly tongues without interpretation is in fact only half a gift, so prophecy without evaluation is in effect only half a gift.[86]

"AND THE SPIRITS OF THE PROPHETS ARE SUBJECT TO THE PROPHETS" (1 COR. 14:32)

When I was the rector of Truro Episcopal Church in Fairfax, Virginia (1976–1989) we had a "Prayer and Praise" service on Friday evenings in which many of the gifts of the Spirit were often manifested. On Sunday mornings, they were occasionally evident, but much less so. On one Sunday, however, during the Prayers of the People, a woman whom I had never previously seen began a very beautiful "prophecy." It was an expression of love and care from the Lord to his people gathered.

But it continued for a very long time, uncomfortably long, and as it continued, the woman's voice became increasingly louder until she was nearly shouting. I was kneeling at a prayer desk inside the altar rail with a microphone next to me. I leaned into the microphone and said, "Let us be quiet before the Lord." The woman stopped.

After the service, several of our teenagers thanked me and said they had been very disturbed by what was happening. That evening,

---

85 George Mallone, *Those Controversial Gifts* (Downers Grove: InterVarsity Press, 1983), 45.

86 James D. G. Dunn, "According to the Spirit of Jesus," in *Theological Renewal*, no. 5 (February–March 1977), 17.

this same woman came to a special program we were having, and she sought me out. She said, "I want to thank you for stopping me. I began in the Spirit, and I ended in the flesh."

CHAPTER 15

DISCERNMENT OF SPIRITS

"To another the discernment of spirits."

—1 CORINTHIANS 12:10

MANY PEOPLE USE the phrase "the gift of discernment," by which they seem to be speaking of a high degree of wisdom and sensitivity in sorting out situations and weighing others' character. No doubt Jesus had all of this, but in the 1 Corinthians list of gifts, Paul next mentions "discernment *of spirits*." This is much more focused.

In chapter 11, we noted that Jesus healed people in two quite distinct ways. He sometimes ministered to a sufferer with the (supernatural) equivalent of a medical healing, as for instance when he relieved Peter's mother-in-law of her fever or when he restored Malchus's ear. But other times he "rebuked" or "cast out" a "demon" (Matt. 17:18) or an "unclean spirit" (Mark 1:26) or a "spirit of infirmity" (Luke 13:11, RSV).

Clearly, these are very specific illustrations of the discernment of spirits. Two equal and opposite errors could lead to medical and spiritual disaster—either *treating a medical problem as if it were a matter of demonic activity* or *treating demonic activity as if it were a medical problem* could lead to catastrophe.

As Matthew tells the story of the epileptic boy, the father kneels before Jesus and implores his mercy. He names his son's condition as epilepsy (a medical condition), and he says, "I brought him to your disciples, but they could not cure him" (Matt. 17:16). The language up to this point makes it sound like the boy has a physical illness. But Jesus "rebuked the demon, and it came out of him, and the boy was cured instantly" (Matt. 17:18). As we saw earlier, Jesus's authority to cast out the demon was in contrast to his disciples' inability to do so because of their "little faith" (Matt. 17:20).[87]

Jesus's anger flashes twice in this story, first at the crowd (not just his disciples who were unable to deal with the situation even though he had commissioned them to cure diseases and cast out spirits[88]): "You faithless and perverse generation, how much longer must I be with you? How much longer must I put up with you?" (Matt. 17:17).

Previously he had called them an "adulterous and sinful generation" (Mark 8:38). Now he adds "faithless and perverse." Shortly, he will tell the disciples that they, in particular, have "little faith" (Matt. 17:20). And then he rebukes the spirit itself: "You spirit that keeps this boy from speaking and hearing, I command you, come out of him, and never enter him again" (Mark 9:25).

Many ancient peoples believed that *all* epilepsy—and many other medical problems—were caused by demonic activity. Today we are very much aware that is *not* the case, and some have moved to the opposite conclusion: that there is no such thing as demonic activity. That is a very dangerous conclusion to draw!

A dictionary definition of epilepsy is: "any of various disorders marked by disturbed electrical rhythms of the central nervous system and typically manifested by convulsive attacks usually with clouding of consciousness."[89]

It was precisely the exercise of the gift of the discernment of spirits that enabled Jesus to perceive that in *this instance* what appeared to be a medical problem was, in fact, a matter of demonic activity.

On another occasion, Jesus said, "If it is by the Spirit of God that

---

87　Eugene Boring comments, "Matthew has condensed a vivid exorcism story, stripping it of its colorful details and reducing it to its bare essentials. Matthew has no interest in the exorcism as such, but uses the healing story to set the stage for the saying on the power of faith." M. Eugene Boring, "The Gospel of Matthew," 368.

88　When the seventy returned from their mission, they exclaimed, "Lord, in your name even the demons submit to us!" (Luke 10:17). But not this time.

89　*Merriam-Webster Collegiate Dictionary*, 10th ed., s.v. "epilepsy."

I cast out demons, then the kingdom of God has come to you" (Matt. 12:28). Sometimes it was obvious to everyone that demons were afflicting people. The swineherds saw what happened to their pigs when Jesus came to the country of the Gadarenes. They "ran off, and on going into the town, they told the whole story about what had happened to the demoniacs" (Matt. 8:33). But Jesus knew what he was dealing with when no one else could discern it.

Is this still a gift for today? Our answer, obviously, depends on whether or not we believe such beings exist!

On the eve of the 1978 Lambeth Conference of Anglican Bishops, the then Bishop of Singapore, Ban It Chu, made this comment: "The contribution of the Church in the Third World will be to reintroduce us to spiritual warfare."[90]

Discernment of spirits enables us to know what we are dealing with, and if we are dealing with "evil" spirits, we have the authority to expel them in Jesus's name. *Nowhere in Scripture is exorcism called a gift of the Holy Spirit.* In Jesus's ministry, it was a matter of his own authority and the anointing of the Spirit; and in the case of his disciples, it was (and is) an authority entrusted to them in his name (Luke 10:17).[91] But knowing whether one is dealing with illness or what may appear to be an illness but is actually caused by demonic activity is an absolute prerequisite to exercising that authority correctly. Again, this is a very specific use of the gift.

The New Testament uses the phrase more widely.

Mallone comments:

> In the Corinthian list of spiritual gifts Paul places prophecy next to the "distinguishing of spirits" (*diakriseis pneumaton*). *Distinguishing* of spirits finds its root in the word for judging (*diakrino*) used in 1 Corinthians 14:29 ["Let two or three prophets speak, and let the others weigh (or judge, or discern) what is

---

90   Ban It Chu, address to the Anglican International Conference on Spiritual Renewal, July 1978.

91   See also the longer ending of Mark, 16:17.

said."] This indicates that distinguishing of spirits is a complementary gift to prophecy as interpretation is to glossolalia.[92]

John wrote in his First Letter, "Beloved, do not believe every spirit, but test the spirits to see whether they are from God; for many false prophets have gone out into the world. By this you know the Spirit of God: every spirit that confesses that Jesus Christ has come in the flesh is from God, and every spirit that does not confess Jesus is not from God" (1 John 4:1–3).

In worship services, then, and wherever else it might occur, when prophecy is given, there is to be discernment. This is both a matter of some having the spiritual gift of discernment of spirits *and* a matter of asking pointed questions: do you confess that Jesus Christ has come in the flesh?

Jesus said there would be prophecies, exorcisms, and miracles performed in his name by some to whom he will declare, "I never knew you; go away from me, you evildoers" (Matt. 7:23).

A notable instance of this occurs in the Book of Acts when "a group of itinerant exorcists (seven sons of a Jewish priest called Sceva) who attempt 'to use the name of Jesus'—just as Paul did—find themselves embarrassingly discomfited by a wicked, yet perceptive, spirit who knows the authority of both Jesus and Paul better than they do (Acts 19:13–16)."[93] Luke tells us, "When this became known to all residents of Ephesus, both Jews and Greeks, everyone was awestruck; and the name of the Lord Jesus was praised" (Acts 19:17). Many became believers and gave up their occult and magical practices.

ELISE

In 1974, I was the chaplain of a preparatory school in Connecticut. A deeply troubled young woman named Elise arrived at our apartment. She said she had been living with her boyfriend in a nearby college town. He kicked her out, and she had no place to go. Somehow she

---

92 Mallone, *Those Controversial Gifts*, 45.

93 F. Scott Spencer, "Exorcism," in *The New Interpreter's Dictionary of the Bible*, vol. 2, 385.

had heard about us, and she hoped we would take her in. We agreed to do so, and she lived with us for several weeks.

Karen and I shared the gospel with her, and she said she wanted to accept Christ, but something was holding her back. Something was hindering her. She said her mother was a practicing witch, and she herself had been involved with occult practices. But even as we prayed for her, there was no breakthrough, no joy, and no liberty in her spirit. She remained deeply agitated.

We were attending a charismatic Presbyterian church at the time, and we shared our concerns about this woman with the two pastors. They agreed with us that it could be a matter of demonic influence. They said they had not had a great deal of experience dealing with this sort of thing, but there was a couple in their congregation who were spiritually mature, who had dealt with similar situations several times, and they thought this couple might be able to help.

We discussed the matter with them, prayed about it, and agreed that we would invite Elise to meet with the four of us. We would counsel her and pray for her, and if we discerned the need, we would ask the Lord to set her free from any demonic oppression. She agreed to meet with us, and we all agreed we would pray and fast beforehand.[94]

It turned out to be a lengthy, loving, prayerful time of ministry, and the man leading us did discern the need to command an evil spirit to leave this young woman. There was no external manifestation, but quite suddenly her agitated spirit was at peace, and she exclaimed, "I am free!" She was then able to commit her life to Christ, and I baptized her in my living room. She has had no relapses, and she is long since a happily married wife and mother.

The man who led our team that day is now the canon theologian of the American Cathedral of the Holy Trinity in Paris.

---

94 In the story of the epileptic boy, some ancient authorities add a verse: "But this kind does not come out except by prayer and fasting" (Matt. 17:21).

CHAPTER 16

TONGUES AND INTERPRETATION

*"To another various kinds of tongues, to
another the interpretation of tongues."*

—I CORINTHIANS 12:10

WITH THE RISE of the Pentecostal and charismatic movements in the twentieth century, a disproportionate amount of attention, both pro and con, has been focused on the last two of the gifts of the Spirit mentioned in this first list of gifts (and they clearly go together): speaking in tongues and the interpretation of tongues.

Thus far, we have seen all of the other gifts mentioned in that list manifested in the life and ministry of Jesus himself. In observing his ministry, we discover what the gifts "look like," and perhaps we will be encouraged by his example to dare to believe that God may wish to give one or more of these same gifts to us.

When we come to speaking in tongues and the interpretation of tongues, we lack any definite example from Jesus's ministry. There simply is no certain evidence, one way or the other, as to whether he had, or used, either or both of these gifts. At least one biblical scholar has ventured the opinion that he had to have prayed in tongues, *"because it is simply impossible to sustain a whole night of prayer otherwise* [as we are told he did in Luke 6:12]."[95] But that remains an opinion.

---

95   Kenneth E. Bailey, remarks at a clergy conference in the Diocese of Central Florida,

(I will argue that it is *probable* that Jesus used these gifts for reasons that will become clear as we unfold this chapter.)

When we examine instances of speaking in tongues in the Book of Acts, and when we read Paul's lengthy discussion of prophecy, tongues, and interpretation in 1 Corinthians 14, we can begin to see several distinct purposes for these related gifts.

The initial occurrence of speaking in tongues was on the Day of Pentecost, when "they were all together in one place" (presumably the same approximately 120 persons mentioned in the previous chapter): "And suddenly from heaven there came a sound like the rush of a violent wind, and it filled the entire house where they were sitting. Divided tongues, as of fire, appeared among them, and a tongue rested on each of them. All of them were filled with the Holy Spirit and began to speak in other languages, as the Spirit gave them ability" (Acts 2:1–4).

It is commonly supposed that they were gathered in the upper room where they had shared the Last Supper with Jesus and where he met the eleven on Easter evening.

That seems very unlikely, in that Luke tells us that while they were waiting for "what my Father promised" (Luke 24:49) "they were *continually in the temple* blessing God" (Luke 24:53). And on the Day of Pentecost, in particular, a day on which all able-bodied Jewish men were *commanded* to be at the festival, it seems most probable they were in the temple again.

Jesus often met with his disciples in a part of the temple called Solomon's Portico (John 10:23), and we know they met there on other occasions after Pentecost (Acts 3:11; 5:12). Either the Portico, or the temple itself, could be called a "house" (the "House of God"). Certainly if all this commotion took place anywhere in the temple, it would quickly draw a crowd!

It is often said that the expatriate Jews from the sixteen nations that are mentioned in Acts 2 heard the disciples *preaching* to them in their own native languages. That is not what the text says. The

October 1996.

"bewildered, amazed, and astonished" crowd asked, "Are not all these who are speaking Galileans? And how is it that we hear, each of us, in our own native language? ... *We hear them speaking about God's deeds of power*" (Acts 2:7–11).

They were not *preaching;* they were *praising.* They were addressing God, thanking and praising him for his wondrous works, no doubt in terms very like what we find in so many of the psalms.[96] Only they were doing so in the native languages of this crowd from many nations. "All were amazed and perplexed, saying to one another, 'What does this mean?'" (Acts 2:12).

Had the disciples been *preaching,* no one would have asked this question. The preaching would have been self-explanatory.

The preaching *began* in answer to their question, "How is it we are hearing them speak in our native languages?" Peter powerfully articulated the gospel, called his listeners to repent and be baptized, and promised that they, too, would receive the same gift of the Holy Spirit, and approximately three thousand people were added to the infant church.

This, then, is the first purpose of the gift of speaking in tongues. It is a vehicle of *praise.* Paul said, "I will sing praise with the spirit, but I will sing praise with the mind, also" (1 Cor. 14:15).

There is a good deal of controversy as to whether the other instances of speaking in tongues recorded in the Book of Acts, were, like this first one, known languages or whether they were essentially "ecstatic utterances." Along with the New English Bible, at least four other translations have used this term: Barclay, Goodspeed, Wand, and Williams. There is also controversy as to whether Paul's phrase about speaking "in the tongues of mortals *and of angels*" (1 Cor. 13:1) refers to real languages not of this world.

---

96 That they were *praising* God rather than *preaching* is also reflected in Peter's comments after the Holy Spirit "fell upon" Cornelius and his household in Acts 10. Luke records that "the circumcised believers who had come with Peter were astounded that the gift of the Holy Spirit had been poured out even on the Gentiles, for they heard them speaking in tongues *and extolling God*." Peter said that their experience was the same as what had happened on the Day of Pentecost: "Can anyone withhold the water for baptizing these people who have received the Holy Spirit *just as we have?*" (Acts 10:44–47).

For our purposes, it does not really matter. As a vehicle of *praise*, tongues are languages and/or ecstatic speech in which we address ourselves to God to glorify him other than in our own known language. Tongues are like another channel of communication with God, one that is not limited to our understanding or our vocabulary.

Why would we want to praise God in a language we do not understand? Robert Tuttle, a leader in the United Methodist Church, gives us his answer:

> There are times in my devotional life when I can no longer find words to express my "innards." ... At that point I allow the Holy Spirit to pray through me in a language that I did not learn. Believe me, I know what it means to learn a language. I struggle with the biblical languages every day....I say a language because I believe it to be a language. My vocabulary is growing. I know enough about language to be able to identify sentence structure. My unknown tongue or prayer language has periods, commas, and exclamation points. It is a marvelous gift.[97]

Rosemary Attlee asked:

> How can I describe this heart language of the spirit but as a love language for the Father's ear? An intimate language springing to the lips in times of pain, grief and fear, as well as joy.... It is not only a superb piece of practical equipment, but in its use there seems to be a pervasive and wholesome aroma of the Holy Spirit, a fragrance my spirit breathes in.[98]

The second purpose of speaking in tongues is for *intercession*. Paul says, "I will pray with the spirit, but I will pray with the mind, also" (1 Cor. 14:15). In Romans, he writes, "The Spirit helps us in our weakness; for we do not know how to pray as we ought, but that very Spirit intercedes with sighs too deep for words. And God, who searches the heart, knows what is the mind of the Spirit, because the Spirit intercedes for the saints according to the will of God" (Rom. 8:26–27).

---

97   Robert G. Tuttle, *The Partakers* (Nashville: Abingdon Press, 1974), 82.
98   Rosemary Attlee, *Renewal*, October/November 1984.

Sighs too deep to be uttered sometimes give way to intercession in tongues that is not bound by our understanding (or lack thereof) of what to pray for and how to pray it.

Interestingly, Mark records two instances of Jesus sighing. The first was when he healed the deaf man with the speech impediment: "[Jesus] looking up to heaven, sighed and said to him 'Ephphatha,' that is, 'be opened.'" (Mark 7:34). The second was when the Pharisees demanded a sign: "And he sighed deeply in his spirit, and said, 'Why does this generation ask for a sign? Truly I tell you, no sign will be given to this generation'" (Mark 8:12).

Why would Mark record this little detail? What is significant about Jesus sighing?

Could either, or both, of these sighs be examples of what Paul described to the Romans—the Spirit interceding with sighs too deep for words? Is it possible that Jesus's sighs gave way to prayer in tongues? We do not know the answer to either of those questions, but they seem worth pondering!

There is disagreement among scholars as to what "Ephphatha" actually meant. Donahue and Harrington have this comment regarding it:

> A few authors claim that this is the Greek vocalization of a Hebrew *niphal* imperative, but most see it as the vocalization of the Aramaic, *eppatha*, the imperative of *petah* ("open"). Though the use of foreign words (*rhesis barbarike*) as an incantation is a frequent motif in magical papyri and in exorcisms, such words often take the form of unintelligible "abracadabras." Whatever the function of the Aramaic term in the pre-Markan tradition, Mark makes it intelligible through his translation ("Be opened"), so that it serves as a word of power that frees the man from his infirmity rather than as a mysterious magical incantation.[99]

A "word of power": is it possible that what actually happened at this point was that Jesus spoke in tongues? Again, we do not know, but it is an intriguing possibility.

---

99 John R. Donahue and Daniel J. Harrington, "The Gospel of Mark," in *Sacra Pagina,* vol. 2 (Collegeville: Liturgical Press, 2002), 240.

Paul Yonggi Cho, pastor of the world's largest congregation in Seoul, Korea, said of his own prayer life:

> Sometimes I feel a burden of prayer: yet I may not know exactly what I should pray for; or I may not have exactly the words to express what I feel. This is the time when I enter my spiritual language and can pierce through my natural inability to articulate to God what I am feeling.[100]

Paul expressly directs his readers in Ephesians to "pray in the Spirit at all times in every prayer and supplication" (Eph. 6:18).

The third use of tongues is in corporate worship when they are accompanied by interpretation. Tongues plus interpretation of tongues becomes a vehicle whereby *God speaks to—or at least blesses or "edifies"—those who hear what is said:*

> Those who speak in a tongue do not speak to other people but to God; for nobody understands them, since they are speaking mysteries in the Spirit. On the other hand, those who prophesy speak to other people for their upbuilding and encouragement and consolation. Those who speak in a tongue build up themselves, but those who prophesy build up the church. Now I would like all of you to speak in tongues, but even more to prophesy. *One who prophesies is greater than one who speaks in tongues, unless someone interprets, so that the church may be built up.*
> —1 Corinthians 14:2–5, emphasis added

Tongues are nowhere in scripture called "the least of the gifts" (as is commonly and disparagingly alleged), but Paul is very clear that if they are not accompanied by interpretation they benefit, or "edify" (RSV), only the tongue-speaker. But *if there is an interpretation accompanying the tongue-speaking, this combination gift becomes the equivalent of prophecy.*

Thus, speaking in tongues can be a vehicle of *praise* (and/or *thanksgiving*),[101] and, when it is accompanied by interpretation, it

---

100 Cited by Pytches, *Come, Holy Spirit*, 65.

101 "If you say a blessing with the spirit, how can anyone in the position of an outsider say the 'Amen' to your thanksgiving since the outsider does not know what you are saying?" (1 Cor. 14:16).

becomes the equivalent of *prophecy,* by which the church is "built up" (1 Cor. 14:5).

So, Paul exhorts the tongue-speaker to pray for the power to interpret (1 Cor. 14:13). And, he says, "If there is no one to interpret, let [the tongue-speakers] be silent and speak to themselves and to God" (1 Cor. 14:28).

Speaking in tongues, along with its sister gift, the interpretation of tongues, has been a source of great controversy and division in the twentieth century (just as it was in the first!).

"The distinct doctrine of the Pentecostal churches," writes Donald Gee, "[is] that speaking in tongues is the 'initial evidence' of the baptism in the Holy Spirit. This article of belief is now incorporated in the official doctrinal schedules of practically all Pentecostal denominations."[102]

We thoroughly reject that position, believing that tongues and the interpretation of tongues are simply two of the many gifts of the Holy Spirit, neither essential nor initial.

However, we want to acknowledge that for many people, speaking in tongues does have a kind of preparatory quality. As they *experience* the Holy Spirit speaking through their own lips, they begin to learn to recognize him when he is prompting them to receive or develop another of his gifts.

I have known only one person who had the gift of interpretation who did not first have the gift of speaking in tongues. Most of the people who frequently prophesy begin doing so only after they have spoken in tongues. Daring to believe God might be able to use us in some of the more dramatic areas of ministry, like healing or even the working of miracles, may be greatly strengthened by the experience of speaking in tongues. It is not a necessary prerequisite, but for many it is a kind of spiritual "training ground" for moving into other gifts and ministries of the Holy Spirit.

So, I want to offer a very tentative opinion: if speaking in tongues

---

102   Cited by Frederick Dale Bruner, *A Theology of the Holy Spirit* (Grand Rapids: Eerdmans, 1970), 76.

is a vehicle of *praise*, and a vehicle of *intercession*, and if Paul can write, "I would like all of you to speak in tongues," and if he can say of himself, "I thank God that I speak in tongues more than all of you" (1 Cor. 14:18), and if he can instruct us to "pray in the Spirit at all times in every prayer and supplication" (Eph. 6:1), *it seems to me a distinct probability that Jesus used this gift.*

He, of all people, *praised* his Father. He, of all people *prayed* for others. If this gift would enable him to do those things better than he could without it, is it not likely that God would give it to him?

And if Paul instructs that those who have the gift of speaking in tongues should pray for the power to interpret, no doubt Jesus would have done that, as well.

LARRY AND DORI

A couple in my parish in Fairfax, Virginia, were very much in love, but she was a believer in Jesus, and he was a non-observant Jew. God gave her the gift of a "prayer language" that she used in her private devotions. One afternoon, she was singing in tongues, thinking herself alone in the house. Her husband walked into the kitchen, and demanded to know, "Where did you learn that?"

She told him she honestly did not know what she was singing; it was a gift from the Holy Spirit. "Well," he said, "you may not know what you are singing, but I do. It is perfect Hebrew."

And he was converted that very moment.

I know clergy who have spoken in international meetings where they did not know the language they were speaking, but (some of) the others present did because it was their native language. And they were blessed by what was said.

And the present president of Oral Roberts University told me he was supernaturally given the ability to speak Spanish *with understanding* though he never studied the language.[103]

---

103   Dr. Mark Rutland, in a personal conversation.

A LETTER FROM BISHOP M'PANGO

On the eve of his consecration in 1981, I prayed with Bishop Gerard M'Pango, the now retired bishop of Western Tanganyika in Tanzania, as we sat together in his car overlooking the diocesan compound. I prayed that he might be filled with the Spirit as he began his new responsibilities. I said, "Just open your mouth and praise the Lord—but not in English or Swahili!" He literally *exploded* in tongues of praise that went on for perhaps fifteen or twenty minutes.

On the day after Pentecost 2011, I received an email from him[104] that said in part:

> Yesterday I went to worship at Christ the King Church here in San Diego, California. Because it was a Pentecost Sunday, when I was given time to greet the church, I took the opportunity to share my spiritual experience at the eve before the day of my consecration 30 years ago. Do you still remember that, John? Do you remember how I shook that car during the infilling of the Holy Spirit and the speaking in tongues? That was the most edifying spiritual experience in my life. All my gifts of leadership, etc., took off from there. That is why I was able to grow my diocese up to 500 congregations and over half a million members by God's grace. After working for 20 years, we had to elect three more assistant bishops to assist me. By the time I took early retirement last year, the diocese had already been divided into 3 more dioceses of Tabora, Shinyanga, and Sumbawanga. That has all happened because of your prayer that afternoon, Saturday before my consecration. So, thank you very much, my brother, for what you did that day for me. When I shared this the congregation erupted into a thunder of applause. Praise the Lord.

Actually, I did nothing. The Holy Spirit did it all.

---

104   Bishop Gerard M'Pango, personal e-mail sent to the author, June 13, 2011. Used with permission.

CHAPTER 17

A Second List of Gifts

"Now you are the body of Christ and
individually members of it."

—1 Corinthians 12:27

A LL OF THE gifts on the first list are clearly and distinctly supernatural in character. And all but tongues and the interpretation of tongues are best illustrated by the ministry of Jesus (who may or may not have used these last two gifts as well).

Following this first list of gifts, Paul elaborates on his favorite metaphor for the church. It is like a human body, with different parts of the body having different functions, and each one needing all the others. He sums up by saying, "Now you [collectively] are the body of Christ and individually members of it" (1 Cor. 14:27).

He then gives the Corinthians a second list of *eight gifts God has given to the church.* This is the only place in the New Testament where gifts are enumerated: first, second, third, then, and so on. And following this list, he asks a series of seven rhetorical questions about six of the gifts he has just mentioned and one he has not. It is clear from the context that all of the questions are to be answered in the negative: no, not all are called to any one ministry or function in the body of Christ, but some are.

> God has appointed in the church first apostles, second prophets, third teachers, then deeds of power, then gifts of healing, forms

of assistance, forms of leadership, various kinds of tongues. Are all apostles? Are all prophets? Are all teachers? Do all work miracles? Do all possess gifts of healing? Do all speak in tongues? Do all interpret?

—1 CORINTHIANS 14:28–30

Paul is not at all consistent in speaking about the *person exercising the gift* or the *gift being exercised*. It is clear that for there to be "deeds of power" (the working of miracles), there has to be someone who performs the miracles. For there to be "forms of assistance" and "forms of leadership," there have to be assistants and leaders. For there to be "various kinds of tongues," there must be tongue-speakers.

- First apostles: Are all apostles? [No]

- Second prophets: Are all prophets? [No]

- Third teachers: Are all teachers? [No]

- Then deeds of power: Do all work miracles? [No]

- Then gifts of healing: Do all possess gifts of healing? [No]

- Forms of assistance

- Forms of leadership

- Various kinds of tongues: Do all speak in tongues? [No]

- Do all interpret? [No]

He asks no question about forms of assistance or leadership, but he does ask about interpretation, which he had not included in the immediately preceding list.

We can make several observations at this point. First, again it is clear that neither here nor anywhere else is Paul (or anyone else) attempting to give an exhaustive and complete list of all the gifts of the Spirit. Everywhere there is a list, it is as if the author is saying, "Now, here are some of the gifts; these are what the gifts of the Spirit are like."

Second, this list includes four gifts that Paul did not mention in his earlier list of nine charisms: apostles, teachers, assistants, and leaders. All four of these seem to be persons holding recognized offices in the church (or at least quasi-offices).

Third, it leaves out four gifts that were in the previous list: the utterance of wisdom, the utterance of knowledge, faith, and the discernment of spirits. The first three of these gifts, the only ones that are enumerated—apostles, prophets, and teachers—are *foundational* to the church. Writing to the Ephesians, Paul said, "So then you are no longer strangers and aliens, but you are citizens with the saints and also members of the household of God, *built upon the foundation of the apostles and prophets*, with Christ Jesus himself as the cornerstone" (Eph. 2:19–20).[105]

Paul called himself an apostle in nearly all of his letters,[106] and in his second letter to the Corinthians he said that in his ministry, "the signs of a true apostle were performed among you with utmost patience, signs and wonders and mighty works" (2 Cor. 12:12). His calling as an apostle *included* the working of miracles and (as we know from the Book of Acts) healings.[107]

Raymond Collins wrote:

---

105   See also Revelation 21:14.

106   He did not use the term in either of his letters to the Thessalonians, though he described his ministry as an apostle in some detail in 1 Thessalonians.

107   Cf. the instantaneous healing of a man from Lystra who had never walked (Acts 14:8ff).

The enumeration draws attention to the role of the apostle as one who preaches the gospel and thereby brings the community into being as a community of believers.... "Apostles" *per se* might simply connote delegates who are sent on a mission (cf. 1 Corinthians 16:3, 4). Paul's use of the term with reference to himself ([and] Apollos and Barnabas), along with his extensive reflection on his foundational role with respect to the church of God at Corinth, supports the idea that in 12:28 "apostle" has, nonetheless, more or less the meaning that Christians generally assign to it.[108]

An apostle is a "sent out one," and while Jesus is never called an apostle, he repeatedly said that he was "sent" by the Father:

- "Whoever welcomes you welcomes me, and whoever welcomes me welcomes the one who sent me" (Matt. 10:40).

- "The Spirit of the Lord is upon me...he has sent me" (Luke 4:18).

- "I must proclaim the good news of the kingdom of God to the other cities also; for I was sent for this purpose" (Luke 4:43).

- "God did not send the Son into the world to condemn the world, but that in order that the world might be saved through him" (John 3:17).

- "My food is to do the will of him who sent me and to complete his work" (John 4:34).

- "Very truly, I tell you, anyone who hears my word and believes him who sent me has eternal life, and does not come under judgment, but has passed from death to life" (John 5:24).

---

108 Raymond F. Collins, "First Corinthians," in *Sacra Pagina*, vol. 7 (Collegeville: Liturgical Press, 1999), 468–469.

With these and many other such statements, Jesus made it absolutely clear that he was *the* "sent out one," and on Easter evening he said to the ten (Judas having killed himself and Thomas being absent), *"As the Father has sent me, so I send you"* (John 20:21). *Their* being sent was part of *his* being sent. *Their* apostleship was part of *his* apostleship.

Professor Ian Siggins summarized the gospel in an intriguing and unique way:

> He was sent.
>
> He was sent to say that he was sent.
>
> He was sent to say that he was sent for us.
>
> We are sent.
>
> We are sent to say that he was sent.
>
> We are sent to say that he was sent for us.[109]

In this second list of gifts, Paul has moved from *manifestations* of the Holy Spirit to *ministries* of the Holy Spirit (even recognized offices) in the church. Anyone open to the Spirit might, for instance, give *a word of prophecy* ("you can all prophesy, one by one" [1 Cor. 14:31]). That is not the same thing as being one who prophesies regularly and who comes to be recognized by others as *a prophet*. Anyone who prays might occasionally be used by God to effect a wonderful *healing*. That is not the same thing as having an established, recognized, and reliable ministry of healing and being recognized by others as a *healer*.

We have just rehearsed the argument that, even though the title is never given to him, Jesus was *the* apostle who sent out other apostles. We saw in chapter 14 that Jesus was *the* prophet whose gifts to his church "were that some would be...prophets," as Paul put it to the

---

109 Ian D. K. Siggins, *Lectures in Church History*, fall semester, Yale Divinity School, 1964.

Ephesians (Eph. 4:11). It is clear that Jesus understood himself to also be *the* teacher who would give to his church other teachers, as well.

"A disciple is not above the teacher, nor a slave above the master. It is enough for the disciple to be like the teacher, and the slave like the master" (Matt. 10:24). "You are not to be called rabbi, for you have one teacher, and you are all students" (Matt. 23:8). "You call me Teacher and Lord—and you are right, for that is what I am" (John 13:13).

As we move to the category of teacher, there is another observation to be made.

There are superb teachers, both Christians and others, who *seem* to come by their ability to teach "naturally." They tried teaching (whatever their subject), found they were good at it, continued teaching, and got better at it. Two intriguing questions would be:

- At what point is the ability to teach deemed to be a gift of the Holy Spirit?

- And, is it possible for someone who is not a Christian to receive a gift of the Spirit?

King David said to the Lord, "*All things* come from you, and of your own have we given you" (1 Chron. 29:14). And James, the brother of Jesus, wrote, "Every generous act of giving, with *every perfect gift*, is from above, coming down from the Father of lights, with whom there is no variation or shadow due to change" (James 1:17).

What we typically call a "natural talent"—whether it is the ability to teach, to sing, to paint, or whatever—must be recognized as a gift from God, even if the person who has that talent does not even believe in God! We typically call people with significant talents "gifted." Well, where do we think the gifting came from? The ability to teach is certainly a gift of the Holy Spirit whenever it is received. Those who are "naturally" good teachers may at some point become believers and recognize that it was God who had so gifted them (and perhaps what they teach will begin to change!).

Paul mentions teaching as a charism only here in 1 Corinthians 14 and Ephesians 4:11, where teachers, along with apostles, prophets, evangelists, and pastors are among Christ's gifts to his church.

Collins writes, "This gift is distinct from the apostolate, preaching, and prophesying. The teacher is one who instructs with regards to God's will, whether in catechesis (cf. 14:9) or as an interpreter of the Scriptures."[110]

Thus far, all of the gifts we have considered were either definitely manifested in Jesus's ministry, or—in the case of tongues and interpretation—we have argued that they were probably manifested in his ministry.

The roles of leaders and helpers are a good deal more difficult to specify. One wonders why Paul did not use terms that he used elsewhere, like *overseer* (Gk. *episkopos*) and *servant* (Gk. *diakonos*). Collins makes the suggestion that *helpers* may have been the term used by the Corinthians to designate those who were involved in taking up the collection on behalf of the saints in Jerusalem, and *leaders* may have been those who hosted the house churches and/or those who presided at the celebrations of the Eucharist.[111]

Or they may have been more general terms as we use them today. In any case, one more observation is in order. We have noted that all of the gifts in the first list had a distinctly supernatural quality to them. The second list includes five gifts that were on that supernatural list (prophecy, miracles, healings, speaking in tongues, and interpretation). But alongside these are ministries that have more the character of offices in the church: apostles and teachers. And, as we have just seen, there were leaders and helpers, which do not *sound* very supernatural at all.

The New Testament makes no such distinction.

All of the gifts of the Spirit, whether "manifestations," "ministries," or "offices," are *God's provision for his people to be and do what he is*

---

110 Collins, "First Corinthians," 469.
111 Ibid.

calling them to be and do: "All these are activated by one and the same Spirit, who allots to each one individually just as the Spirit chooses" (1 Cor. 12:11).

Some of the gifts are very dramatic. Others seem almost pedestrian in comparison with them. But Paul writes:

> Indeed, the body does not consist of one member, but of many....God arranged the members in the body, each one of them, as he chose....The members of the body that seem to be weaker are indispensable, and those members of the body that we think less honorable we clothe with greater honor, and our less respectable members are treated with greater respect; whereas our more respectable members do not need this.... If one member suffers, all suffer together with it; if one member is honored, all rejoice together with it.
>
> —1 CORINTHIANS 12:14–26

All of God's gifts are needed; all are to be honored. Whether one is called to be a spectacularly gifted preacher with a ministry of signs and wonders, or whether one is called to do the dishes after coffee hour, we are all members of Christ's body, called and gifted by the Spirit of God to do the things that please him and serve others.

CHAPTER 18

A List Hidden in the Love Chapter

*"Strive for the greater gifts. And I will show
you a still more excellent way."*

—1 Corinthians 12:31

So the gifts of the Spirit are things we should desire, seek, and "strive for." And there is a "more excellent way" of seeking them. That way is the way of *agape* love:

> If I speak in the tongues of mortals and of angels, but do not have love, I am a noisy gong or a clanging cymbal. And if I have prophetic powers, and understand all mysteries and all knowledge, and if I have all faith, so as to remove mountains, but do not have love, I am nothing. If I give away all my possessions, and if I hand over my body to be burned [alternative reading], but do not have love, I gain nothing.
>
> —1 Corinthians 13:1–3

Many commentators have not even recognized that hidden within Paul's sublime description of love is a third list of gifts of the Holy Spirit.

Paul does an extraordinary thing in this chapter. Many times previously in the letter, he has offered himself as an example worthy of emulation.[112] Now he offers himself as a *negative* example: "If *I* speak

---

112   1 Corinthians 2:1–5; 3:10; 4:1–5; 9:1–12, 19–27

in tongues...if *I* have prophetic powers...[if *I*] understand all mysteries and all knowledge...if *I* have all faith...if *I* give away all my possessions...if *I* hand over my body..." (1 Cor. 13:1–3). "*I* am a noisy gong or a clanging cymbal...*I* am nothing...*I* gain nothing" (1 Cor. 13:1–3).

Paul Samply writes:

> This rhetorical device...allows Paul to lay out some stern warnings to his auditors without the risk of unduly offending them and with the added advantage that his application to himself allows, even subtly commends, that others apply the same test to themselves. The auditors can hear much more forceful and blunt criticism of themselves precisely because it is Paul's critique of his imaginary, contrary-to-fact self.[113]

We have noted that this greatly beloved passage of scripture[114] is, in effect, an *interruption* in Paul's discussion of the gifts of the Holy Spirit. As we said previously, it is as if he said, "I cannot go on talking about the gifts without reminding you of the context in which they are to be exercised."

The context for the gifts of the Spirit is that of the fruit of the Spirit. The gifts are for "the common good" (1 Cor. 12:7), for "building up" the church (1 Cor. 14:5). If I exercise the gifts of the Spirit without love for the other members of the church, the gifts may still bless others, but "I" will be absolutely worthless.

Many commentators have not seen Paul's references to "understanding all mysteries" and "having all knowledge" as references back to the gifts he originally named as the "utterance of wisdom" and the "utterance of knowledge." They treat them instead as references to having great wisdom and knowledge generally. If that is what Paul meant, the point about love would be the same, but it would seem a strange departure from what he is clearly doing.

Paul has been discussing the gifts of the Spirit in chapter 12. He

---

113 J. Paul Samply, "First Corinthians," in *The New Interpreter's Bible*, vol. 10 (Nashville: Abingdon, 2002), 952.

114 It is probably the third best known passage in Scripture, after the Lord's Prayer and the Twenty-third Psalm.

will return to that discussion, at the very point he left off, in chapter 14. The point of chapter 13 is to say—as clearly as possible—that *the gifts of the Spirit are not to be exercised apart from the context of love.*

Paul mentions five gifts that by now are familiar to us: tongues, prophecy, wisdom ("understand all mysteries"), knowledge, and faith. With regard to tongues, he adds a phrase that he uses nowhere else: "tongues of men [as on the Day of Pentecost] *and of angels.*"

Note: the only times human beings hear angels speaking in Scripture, *they are speaking in the languages of those human beings* (e.g., the seraphs in Isaiah's vision [Isa. 6] or Gabriel to Mary [Luke 1:26–38]). Perhaps Paul knows (or imagines) that angelic speech is exquisitely lovely and he intends to contrast it with the noisy gong or clanging cymbal of lovelessness.

Collins writes:

> For a striking contrast with angelic speech Paul draws upon the experience of the Corinthians whose economy was to a significant degree dependent upon the manufacture and trading of bronze items. In Paul's day echo chambers, generally made of bronze, were strategically placed in niches around amphitheaters, where they served as effective acoustical devices (cf. Vitruvius, *Architecture* 5.3.8 [ca. 30 BCE]). A loveless Paul and those speaking in tongues without love are comparable to pieces of bronze. They echo sound but they do not resonate the tone of a fine musical instrument (cf. 14:7–8). "I have become sounding brass" (v.1) is parallel with "I am good for nothing" (v. 2) and "it is not to my advantage" (v. 3).[115]

That he is still thinking of gifts of the Spirit is evident in his comment regarding faith—"so as to remove mountains"—which is exactly the same phrase Jesus used when his disciples asked why they had been unable to cast the demon out of the epileptic boy: "Because of your little faith. For truly I tell you, if you have faith the size of a mustard seed, you will say to this mountain, 'Move from here to there,' and it will move; and nothing will be impossible for you" (Matt. 17:20–21).

To all of this, Paul adds two categories that might not seem like

---

115   Collins, "First Corinthians," 473.

"gifts" at all, but once again, if we remember what he is doing in this chapter, they have to be seen as such: "If I give away all I have, and if I deliver my body to be burned" (1 Cor. 13:3, RSV).

There is a major textual problem with this latter phrase, and some translations (including the New Revised Standard Version) render it "so that I may boast." But it seems to be a reference to martyrdom. There is a kind of hierarchical development in these first three verses of the chapter. As we have seen, speaking in tongues, if it is unaccompanied by interpretation, edifies or "builds up" only the one who speaks. Prophecy, words of wisdom and knowledge, and the gift of faith "to remove mountains" are all gifts that can bless others greatly. But going beyond them, I might believe I am called to give away everything I have, as Saint Francis believed he was called to do. And finally, there is giving away even my very self.[116]

Are some believers called to extreme generosity and (therefore) extreme poverty? Yes. Is there a charism from God to enable them to do so? How could they do so otherwise?

Are some called even to martyrdom? Yes. And is there a charism from God even for that? Yes. One thinks of so many Christian martyrs who went cheerfully to their deaths.[117]

---

116 Paul commented to the Romans that, "Indeed, rarely will anyone die for a righteous person—though perhaps for a good person someone might actually dare to die" (Rom. 5:7).

117 Cf. Polycarp, who is reported to have prayed before he was burned at the stake, "Lord God Almighty, Father of your beloved and blessed child Jesus Christ, through whom we have received knowledge of you, God of angels and hosts and all creation, and of the whole race of the upright who live in your presence, I bless you that you have thought me worthy of this day and hour, to be numbered among the martyrs and share in the cup of Christ, for resurrection to eternal life, for soul and body in the incorruptibility of the Holy Spirit. Among them may I be accepted before you today, as a rich and acceptable sacrifice just as you, the faithful and true God, have prepared and foreshown and brought about. For this reason and for all things I praise you, I bless you, I glorify you, through the eternal heavenly high priest Jesus Christ, your beloved child, through whom be glory to you, with him and the Holy Spirit, now and for the ages to come. Amen." See *Holy Men, Holy Women* (New York: Church Publishing, 2010), 238. See also the entry on "The Martyrs of Uganda," page 404, which states: "On June 3, 1886, thirty-two young men, pages at the court of King Mwanga of Buganda, were burned to death at Namugongo for their refusal to renounce Christianity.... The Namugongo Martyrdoms produced a result entirely opposite to Mwanga's intentions. The example of these martyrs, who walked to their death singing hymns and praying for their enemies, so inspired

But Paul's point is that if I do any of these things without love, "*I*" gain nothing:

> Paul has previously urged the Corinthians to consider what is to their own advantage (6:12; 7:35; 10:23, 33; 12:7). Now he offers himself as an example of one who has considered what is to his own advantage and has come to the conclusion that there is no advantage whatsoever that would accrue to himself if he does not have love.[118]

(Many have questioned how Jesus's castigation of the Pharisees and his driving the money-changers in the temple can be reconciled with Paul's—and Jesus's own—call to act always in love. The simple answer is that if we truly love someone we must hate the thing that corrupts and spoils him or her. "Friends don't let friends drive drunk," we are told at holiday seasons. "Take away the keys, call a cab, drive the person home yourself. Risk the friendship for the sake of the friend." Jesus hated what the corruption of the Pharisees and the money-changers was doing to *them* as much as he hated what it was doing to *others*.)

We considered Paul's description of love in chapter 5. Now he contrasts the permanence of love with the transience of the gifts: "Love never ends" (1 Cor. 13:8). But prophecies, tongues, and (words of) knowledge (and, presumably, all the other gifts of the Spirit) are for this age, and when we see our Lord "face to face" (1 Cor. 13:12) they will be needed no longer.

There are two more clues in this final paragraph of the chapter that Paul has been speaking of the gifts of the Spirit throughout. He says in verse 8, "As for knowledge, it will come to an end." But four verses

---

many of the bystanders that they began to seek instruction from the remaining Christians. Within a few years the original handful of converts had multiplied many times and spread far beyond the court. The martyrs had left the indelible impression that Christianity was truly African, not simply a white man's religion. Most of the missionary work was carried out by Africans rather than by white missionaries, and Christianity spread rapidly. Uganda is now the most Christian nation in Africa."

118   Collins, "First Corinthians," 477.

later, he says, "Now I know only in part; then I will know fully, even as I have been fully known."

The *words of knowledge* will come to an end when *knowledge itself* is complete. Similarly, the *gift of faith* (so as to remove mountains) will come to an end when all the gifts cease to function because they are no longer needed. But *faith itself*—knowing God fully, even as I have been fully known—will "abide" along with hope and love.

Our catalogue of gifts of the Spirit is growing, and in surprising directions!

Evidently at least some of the gifts of the Holy Spirit are actually his enabling us to do what God is calling us to do. Different gifts for different Christians, and all within the context of love.

CHAPTER 19

STRIVE FOR THE GIFTS

"Since you are eager for spiritual gifts, strive to excel in them."
—1 CORINTHIANS 14:12

IT IS EVIDENT from Paul's lengthy discussion of tongues, interpretation, and prophecy in 1 Corinthians 14 that many believers in the church in Corinth had allowed their ability to speak in tongues to become a source of pride (and, perhaps, division). Paul is very clear that unless there is someone to interpret (either the tongue-speaker or another), the tongue-speaking should be done in private.

We have already noticed that Paul ends chapter 12 and begins chapter 14 on the same note: "Strive for the greater gifts. And I will show you a still more excellent way" (12:31); "Pursue love and strive for the spiritual gifts, and especially that you may prophesy" (14:1). Now he says it a third time: "Since you are eager for spiritual gifts, strive to excel in them for building up the church" (v. 12).

But how does one *strive* for a *gift?* If there were something one could do to *earn* it, it would not be a *gift.* Striving for something begins with earnestly desiring it, and if I recognize that the thing in question is a gift from God, perhaps that means *asking* him for it.

Jesus said, "Ask, and it will be given you; search, and you will find; knock, and the door will be opened for you....If you then, who are evil, know how to give good gifts to your children, how much more will your Father in heaven give good things to those who ask him!" (Matt. 7:7–11) Luke's version is more to the point: "If you then, who are evil, know how to give good gifts to your children, how much more will the heavenly Father give *the Holy Spirit* to those who ask him!" (Luke 11:13).

Luke places that promise after Jesus teaches his disciples to pray, *asking* God that his kingdom might come and *asking* him for bread each day, the forgiveness of our sins (as we forgive others), and that we might not be brought to the time of trial. He follows that with Jesus's parable of the persistent friend: "I tell you, even though he will not get up and give him anything because he is his friend, at least because of his persistence he will get up and give him whatever he needs" (Luke 11:8).

And then he gives the promise: "The heavenly Father will give the Holy Spirit to those who ask him!" The implication is inescapable: the heavenly Father will give the Holy Spirit to those who ask for him *persistently*.

Jesus told another parable on the same subject, that of the widow and the unjust judge: "Because this widow keeps bothering me, I will grant her justice, so that she may not wear me out by continually coming" (Luke 18:5).

What? Is God like the neighbor who will grant his friend's request only because he will not take no for an answer? Is he like an unjust judge who will grant someone's request only because she keeps bothering him? Of course not! Jesus's point is just the opposite: "And will not God grant justice to his chosen ones who cry to him day and night? Will he delay long in helping them? I tell you, he will *quickly* grant justice to them" (Luke 18:7–8).

God is not like a reluctant friend or an unjust judge; he will *quickly* grant what they ask. But notice: they must "cry to him day and night." They must be *persistent*.

There is a tension here! Time is not the same thing to God as it is to us! Both Old and New Testaments say that "with the Lord one day is like a thousand years, and a thousand years like one day" (2 Pet.

3:8).[119] It may seem to us that we have been praying for something for a very long time, while from God's perspective he is answering our prayer *quickly*.

A teaching in some parts of the church says that we must ask God for something only once. If we ask a second time, it demonstrates we had no confidence or faith that God heard our request the first time. Jesus says the opposite: God will "quickly" answer, but only if we are persistent, only if we cry to him day and night.

So, how long should we pray for something? *Until we get an answer.*

Sometimes the answer will be no. Jesus prayed three times, "If it is possible, let this cup pass from me" (Matt. 26:39, 42, 44). It did not. Paul prayed three times that a thorn in his flesh might be removed (2 Cor. 12:8). God said, instead, "My grace will be sufficient for you to cope with it." (But note: he gave an answer.)

Sometimes the answer will be to wait. L. B. Cowman's classic devotional *Streams in the Desert* has this comment for May 24:

> If God had told Abraham while he was in Haran that he would have to wait thirty years before holding his promised child in his arms, his heart might have failed him. So God, as an act of his gracious love, hid from Abraham the number of weary years he would be required to wait. Only as the time was approaching, with but a few months left to wait, did God reveal his promise: "At the appointed time next year...Sarah will have a son" (Genesis 18:14). The "appointed time" came at last, and soon the joyous laughter that filled the patriarch's home caused the now elderly couple to forget their long and tiring wait.
>
> So take heart, dear child, when God requires you to wait. The One you wait for will not disappoint you. He will never be even five minutes behind "the appointed time." And soon "your grief will turn to joy" (John 16:20).[120]

And sometimes the answer will be yes. But we are to pray until we get an answer. Luke tells us that the *purpose* of the parable about the

---

119 Cf. Psalm 90:4

120 L. B. Cowman, *Streams in the Desert* (Grand Rapids: Zondervan, 1997), 206.

widow and the judge was to tell the disciples *"about their need to pray always and not to lose heart"* (Luke 18:1).

We are to pray for the coming of God's kingdom until it arrives. We are to pray for bread on a daily basis. We are to pray for the forgiveness of our sins as often as we commit them. We are to pray that we not be brought to the time of trial [or testing or temptation]. We are to pray for wisdom, James tells us (James 1:5). We are to "let our requests be known unto God" (Phil. 4:6). And, among other things, *we are to pray for the Holy Spirit.*

But did we not receive the Holy Spirit in baptism and at confirmation? Yes, but we need to receive him on a day-by-day and moment-by-moment basis. In Ephesians, Paul contrasts being filled with the Holy Spirit with being drunk with wine (an obvious allusion to the sneering accusation that the disciples were "filled with new wine" [Acts 2:13] when they were first filled with the Spirit on the Day of Pentecost):

> Do not get drunk with wine, for that is debauchery; but *be filled* (Gk. *plerousthe*) *with the Spirit*, as you sing psalms and hymns and spiritual songs among yourselves, singing and making melody to the Lord in your hearts, giving thanks to God the Father at all times and for everything in the name of our Lord Jesus Christ.
> —EPHESIANS 5:18–20

The command here is with a present passive imperative verb—continuous present tense, it is sometimes called. It could be translated, "be filled, and go on being filled" or—literally—"be being filled with the Spirit." Interestingly, Paul here says that (one of) the way(s) this will happen is as we are "lost in wonder, love, and praise"[121] by *singing.*

Paul mentions three categories of singing: psalms, hymns, and "spiritual songs." Psalms are the *words of God* set to music; hymns are the *words of men and women* (that we hope are in accord with the words of God), again, set to music. And "spiritual songs"—which bears a resemblance to "spiritual gifts"—are *songs given by the Holy*

---

121 Charles Wesley, "Love Divine, All Loves Excelling."

Spirit, singing as the Spirit prompts us, either in our own language or, possibly, in tongues.

So, be filled and go on being filled. Ask for the Holy Spirit persistently, daily, on a moment-by-moment basis. And if we are to "strive for" the spiritual gifts, does that not mean *asking* God to give them, recognizing that he will do so "as the Spirit chooses"? (1 Cor. 12:11).

Paul specifically says that "one who speaks in a tongue should pray for the power to interpret" (1 Cor. 14:13). If I am to "strive for the spiritual gifts and especially that I may prophesy" (1 Cor. 14:1), does that not mean *asking* God to give me that gift?

Placing the discussion of the gifts within the context of love (chapter 13) is a reminder that the purpose of the gifts is to bless others, not ever to become proud of my ability to do a certain thing, no matter how spectacular it may be. This is why if it edifies only myself (speaking in tongues), I am to use it privately. But if it is a channel for blessing to others, I am encouraged to "strive for" it—i.e., to *ask* God for it, be open to receiving it, and willing to use it ("I will pray with the spirit…I will sing praise with the spirit… [I will] say a blessing with the spirit" [1 Cor. 14:15–16]).

People sometimes ask, "What is the best gift?" Paul gives one answer: "especially that you may prophesy"—because a prophecy coming from God blesses and edifies all who hear it.

But another answer is, *"The best gift is the one that is needed at the time."* Healing is a spectacular gift, but if no one is sick it really is not needed. Performing miracles is truly astonishing, but if what is needed is "forms of assistance," miracles may be out of place. Let us ask God for the gifts that are needed.

ASKING GOD TO
EQUIP US FOR MINISTRY

In chapter 15, I recounted the story of ministry to a very troubled young woman who lived with Karen and me back in 1974. Karen and I, along with the other couple from the Presbyterian church, prepared for that time of ministry by praying and fasting.

What I did not include earlier is that up until then, I had been fairly resistant when various friends urged me to "strive for the gifts." I had the sense that God had already given me various ministerial gifts, and if, in his sovereignty, he wished to bestow additional ones, I would welcome them. But I was not going to seek them.

But as I tried to prepare myself for ministry to Elise, I realized we might be dealing with spiritual realities I had never encountered previously. And I found myself saying, "Lord, forgive me for having a hardness of heart toward the more dramatic dimension of your Spirit's working. If it would help in ministering to Elise to be able to pray for her in tongues, then please give me tongues. If it would help for me to have a vision or to speak a word of prophecy or to pronounce healing—or whatever—please give me the gifts that will enable me to be a channel of your ministry to her."

As I prayed, I saw my first vision. (I have not had many!) It was not terribly profound; literally, it was seeing light at the end of a tunnel— a mental image that flashed through my mind. But it was an encouragement! And for the first time in my life, I began praying in tongues.

I have known people whose experience of tongues was dramatic: full blown languages with rich vocabularies (like Bishop M'Pango's, recounted in chapter 16). Mine was not like that. I only received a few phrases (and it has never developed into much more than that). But it did seem to open another channel of communication with God that was not limited by my vocabulary or understanding.

And, as I said in chapter 15, Elise was wonderfully delivered. We need not fear the gifts of God. He gives only good ones.

CHAPTER 20

A Word About Women

*"As in all the churches of the saints, women should be silent
in the churches... they are not permitted to speak."*

—1 Corinthians 14:33

*"There is no longer Jew or Greek, there is no
longer slave or free, there is no longer male and
female; for all of you are one in Christ Jesus."*

—Galatians 3:28

B EFORE LEAVING PAUL'S discussion of tongues, interpretation,
and prophecy in 1 Corinthians, there is a passage that must
be dealt with. We have been assuming thus far that the gifts
of the Spirit are for all of God's children, men and women, boys
and girls, Jews and Gentiles—all who believe in Christ. Paul writes,
"When you come together, *each one* has a hymn, a lesson, a revelation,
a tongue, or an interpretation" (1 Cor. 14:26).

He urges that there be no more than two or three messages in
tongues, and then only if there is interpretation (1 Cor. 14: 27–28). He
urges two or three prophets to speak and let "the others" (presumably
he other prophets, or possibly the whole congregation) weigh what is
said (1 Cor. 14:29). He says that "all things should be done decently
and in order" (1 Cor. 14:40). A steady hand on the tiller is required in
worship services where the gifts of the Spirit are encouraged.

But then, suddenly, there is this completely jarring passage:

> As in the churches of the saints, women should be silent in the churches. For they are not permitted to speak, but should be subordinate, as the law also says. If there is anything they desire to know, let them ask their husbands at home. For it is shameful for a woman to speak in church.[122]
>
> —1 CORINTHIANS 14:33–35

This passage is much debated among New Testament scholars, but the first thing we need to recognize about it is that if it really means what it seems to say, women should not only refrain from prophesying and speaking in tongues and giving interpretations, but should also be excluded from *any* ministry that involves speaking. They must not teach, preach, pray (aloud), read Scripture, sing, or do anything that involves opening their mouths. They are to be *silent*.

But such an absolute prohibition would contradict both the teaching and the practice of the New Testament as a whole, and specifically it would contradict what Paul himself said elsewhere. The immediately preceding paragraph certainly seems to contain an exhortation for *all* Christians to come to worship prepared to offer vocal expressions of praise and instruction. And three chapters earlier, Paul gave detailed instructions regarding the ways in which women *are* to pray and prophesy (1 Cor. 11:1–16).

We need to understand that beginning in 1 Corinthians 7 and continuing for nine chapters, to the end of the letter, Paul was commenting on a number of issues the Corinthians had raised in a letter they wrote to him ("Now concerning the matters about which you wrote…" [1 Cor. 7:1]). Because there is no punctuation in New Testament Greek, it is not always clear where the question leaves off and where the answer begins, but in most cases we can surmise what is inquiry and what is response.

For example, the Corinthians asked Paul to comment on the

---

122   The material that follows in this chapter runs parallel (nearly, but not quite verbatim) to a chapter I wrote in a book entitled *Our Anglican Heritage*, second edition, co-authored with Dr. Sam C. Pascoe, and published by Wipf and Stock Publishers, Eugene, Oregon in 2010; see pages 173–176. Used by permission of Wipf and Stock Publishers. www.wipfandstock.com

statement, "It is well for a man not to touch a woman" (1 Cor. 7:1). His answer comprises the remainder of chapter 7. They inquire as to whether or not "all things are lawful" in chapter 10 and, once again, his response is given in the remainder of that chapter (1 Cor. 10:23ff).

Similarly, it appears that the passage in chapter 14 commanding women to remain silent is something the Corinthians asked Paul to respond to, rather than something he addressed to them. His response was a terse, even angry retort: "What! Did the word of God originate with you, or are you the only ones it has reached?" (1 Cor. 14:36, RSV).

The apostle Paul, so often caricatured as a great hater of women, is actually saying that no such prohibition could possibly be in keeping with the new covenant in which the gifts, graces, and ministries are for *all* of God's children, "your sons and your daughters" (Acts 2:17), male and female alike.

On closer examination, we discover this must be so. What does the phrase "in all the churches of the saints" (1 Cor. 14:33) possibly mean? It appears nowhere else in the New Testament, and on the surface it is redundant. And what "law" is it that says the women are not permitted to speak? *There is no such law in the Old Testament.* Even if there were, Paul's thesis of God's grace is that we are no longer "under the law" anyway. The fact of the matter is that the "law" referred to is the teaching of the Judaizers that only men may receive religious instruction—something that Paul rejected decisively: "What!"

That little particle translated "What!" is a complete disjuncture. It could be translated "Nonsense!" Paul used it repeatedly in 1 Corinthians to express his sharpest disagreement with things being quoted to him.[123]

Gilbert Belezikian notes that:

> The grammatical structure of [verse 36] indicates a sharp break with the preceding statement.... Recent scholarship has called attention to the disjunctive force of the particle *ei* ["What!"] that introduces verse 36.... Moreover, the abrupt shift from the third person pronoun ("they," the women) in the prohibition statement

---

123 1 Cor. 6:1, 2, 9, 16, 19; 9:6, 8, 10; 10:22; 11:13

to an emphatic second-person masculine in verse 36 (*monous*: "just you men") indicates that Paul is now taking to task a male element in the Corinthian church, rather than rebuking women for getting out of line....The rebuke is for their willingness to replace his standards regarding male/female rules with the anti-women proscriptions of the Judaizing teaching.[124]

Once we understand this, we will be able to understand the phrase "in all the churches of the saints." The earliest use of "saints" was for the *Jewish* Christians of Jerusalem and Palestine. When churches were finally established in the Gentile world, the *Jewish* Christians continued to be called "the saints." An example of this is found in 1 Corinthians 16:1: "Now concerning the collection *for the saints.*"

Gradually, "the saints" came to be used for all Christians, but the phrase still had special connotations for the original Jewish converts. Thus, the practice of trying to silence the women was not the universal practice of all the churches, but it was the attempt of the Judaizers to impose yet another law on the new covenant community. This, Paul totally rejected.

One other passage also seems at first to severely limit the ministry of women, 1 Timothy 2:8–15, and especially verses 11 and 12: "Let a woman learn in silence with full submission. I permit no woman to teach or to have authority over a man; she is to keep silent."

A superficial reading of the passage will suggest, again, a radical prohibition against women opening their mouths in church. Once again, we must observe that on the contrary, women did teach, pray, counsel, and prophesy, and that Paul not only instructed them to do so, he used them in such ministries and commended them for their ministries.

The statement is indeed a radical one, but what is radical about it is not that a woman should learn *in silence*, but that she should be permitted to learn *at all*. It was the Jewish culture that forbade women being instructed, as we have just seen. But just as Jesus commended Mary of Bethany for having "chosen the best part" when she broke all

---

124 Gilbert Bilezikian, *Beyond Sex Roles* (Grand Rapids: Baker, 1985), 151–152.

the social mores of her day by seating herself at his feet in the position of a disciple (Luke 10:38–41), so Paul said of women, *"Let them learn."*

The word *authority* in this passage is not the usual Greek word *exousia*, meaning "privilege" or "right," but *authenteo*, meaning "to usurp." In effect, Paul said, "I am not going to permit an uninstructed woman to usurp authority in the church, but I insist that she be discipled for it—in exactly the same way men are."

On the Day of Pentecost, in response to the accusation that the tongue-speakers were "filled with new wine," Peter quoted from the prophecy of Joel, saying:

> This is that of which he spoke: "In the last days it will be, God declares, that I will pour out my Spirit upon all flesh, and your sons *and your daughters* shall prophesy, and your young men shall see visions, and your old men shall dream dreams. Even upon my slaves, both men *and women*, in those days I will pour out my Spirit; and they shall prophesy."
>
> —ACTS 2:16–18

The gifts of the Holy Spirit are for all God's children, thanks be to God.

CHAPTER 21

How Shall We Use
These Gifts?

"We have gifts that differ according to the grace given to us."
—Romans 12:6

M OST SCHOLARS DATE the writing of Paul's first letter to the Corinthians in the spring or summer of 54 A.D. He wrote his letter to the Romans, a very different kind of congregation, from Corinth at the end of the third missionary journey, probably in 57 A.D. Thus, Paul had been able to ponder the mysteries of Christ and the Spirit for an additional three years. When he returned to the theme of the gifts of the Spirit in Romans 12, there were strong echoes of what he said to the Corinthians previously.

Before we examine the passage, let us put it into context.

Romans 11 ends with a great doxology of praise. Paul has been reflecting on the fact that because the majority of the Jews he was attempting to evangelize rejected the message of the gospel, he became "an apostle to the Gentiles" (Rom. 11:13).[125] But, he says, when "the full number of the Gentiles has come in...all Israel will be saved [because] the gifts and the calling of God are irrevocable" (Rom. 11:25, 26, 29). And in this he rejoices:

---

125   See Acts 13:46.

O the depth of the riches and wisdom and knowledge of God!
How unsearchable are his judgments and how inscrutable his
ways! For who has known the mind of the Lord? Or who has
been his counselor? Or who has given a gift to him, to receive a
gift in return? For from him and through him and to him are all
things. To him be the glory forever. Amen.

—ROMANS 11:33–36

He continues in chapter 12: "I appeal to you *therefore...*" [i.e., *because*
God's judgments are unsearchable, his ways inscrutable, *because* his
plan includes the salvation of "the full number of the Gentiles" and
"all Israel"]. "I appeal to you, therefore, brothers and sisters, by the
mercies of God, to present your bodies as a living sacrifice, holy and
acceptable to God, which is your spiritual worship" (Rom. 12:1).

N. T. Wright says:

> The opening two verses of the section are as dense as any passage
> in Paul, and as so often they state concisely a theme that will
> then be unpacked and explored in various different ways. The
> key transition word is "therefore": not the only time Paul draws
> an ethical conclusion in this letter (see, e.g., 6:12; 8:12), but the
> most obvious moment of transition between the two major parts
> of the letter.[126]

Because we, members of the body of Christ, are the recipients of
God's grace, because we have been included in his unsearchable and
inscrutable plan of salvation, our grateful response must be to worship
him by presenting our very bodies as a living sacrifice; that is, yielding
them to him to do with as he wishes.

Archbishop Thomas Cranmer caught this exactly in the *First
Prayer-Book of Edward VI*:

> WHERFORE, O Lorde and heauenly father, according to the
> Instytucyon of thy derely beloued sonne, our sauior Jesu Christ,
> we thy humble seruantes do celebrate, and make here before

---

126   N. T. Wright, "Romans," in *The New Interpreter's Bible*, vol. 10 (Nashville:
Abingdon, 1992), 703.

thy diuine Maiestie, with these thy holy giftes, the memoryall whyche thy sonne hath wylled us to make, hauyng in remembrauce his blessed passion, mightie resurreccyon, and glorious ascencion, rendering unto thee most hartie thankes, for the innumerable benefites procured unto us by the same, entierely desiring thy fatherly goodness, mercifully to accepte this our Sacrifice of praise and thankes geuing: most humbly beseeching thee to graunt, that by the merites and death of thy sone Jesus Christ, and through faith in his bloud, we and al thy whole church, may obteigne remission of our sinnes, and all other benefites of hys passion. And here wee offer and present unto thee (O Lorde) oure selfe, oure soules, and bodies, to be a reasonable, holy, and liuely sacrifice unto thee: humbly besechyng thee, that whosoeuer shalbee partakers of thys holy Communion, maye worthily receiue the most precious body and bloude of thy sonne Jesus Christe: and bee fulfilled with thy grace and heauenly benediccion, and made one bodye with thy sonne Jesu Christe, that he maye dwell in them, and they in hym.

Paul continues, "Do not be *con*formed to this world, but be *trans*formed by the renewing of your mind, so that you may discern what is the will of God—what is good and acceptable and perfect" (Rom. 12:2). J. B. Phillips's memorable translation of the verse was, "Don't let the world around you squeeze you into its own mold, but let God re-mold your minds from within, so that you may prove in practice that the plan of God for you is good, meets all his demands and moves towards the goal of true maturity."

This, then, is the context in which Paul returns to a discussion of the gifts of the Spirit. God has done, and is doing, something spectacular and beyond our imagining in and through his Son. And yet, because we who are believers are *in* his Son, we are part of what he is doing. *Therefore*, we are to join Paul in worshiping God with our entire being, presenting to him our very bodies, and being renewed in our minds, changing from what we were in this world to what we are becoming in Christ.

Paul writes:

> For by the grace given to me I say to everyone among you not to think of yourself more highly than you ought to think, but to think with sober judgment, each according to the measure of faith that God has assigned. For as in one body we have many members, and not all the members have the same function, so we, who are many, are one body in Christ, and individually we are members one of another. We have gifts that differ according to the grace given to us: prophecy, in proportion to faith; ministry, in ministering; the teacher, in teaching; the exhorter, in exhortation; the giver, in generosity; the leader, in diligence; the compassionate, in cheerfulness.
>
> —Romans 12:3–8

Paul previously warned his readers not to "claim to be wiser than you are" (Rom. 11:25). He now urges each and every one of them "not to think of yourself more highly than you ought to think." From what follows, it is clear that he is specifically warning them not to think too highly of the various ministry gifts God has given them and not to become proud of their various functions within the body of Christ.

(Paul recognized that the problems in Corinth—disunity in the body stemming from pride over gifts—could happen anywhere.)

He asserts that he is not addressing them on his own authority, but "by the grace given to me" in his special calling and gifting as an apostle. He says to be transformed by the renewing of your minds, so you will think rightly, and this is how God wants you to think. He has given each of us a place in the body, a ministry and function to be fulfilled. Do not think of whatever role God has given you as being more important than it is. "Think with sober judgment, each according to the measure of faith that God has assigned."

Paul goes on to discuss in chapters 14 and 15 the reality that some are "weak" in faith and others "strong." Should I find myself being "strong" in faith at any point, it is no cause for pride. It was the gift of God in the first place, and I cannot legitimately be proud of something God has given me. Should I find myself "weak" in faith at another point, I would do well to follow the example of the father of the epileptic boy and *ask* for help: "I believe; help my unbelief" (Mark 9:24).

He then lists seven spiritual gifts.

Once again, Paul is not consistent in speaking of the *person exercising the gift* or the *gift being exercised.* He also uses an unusual turn of phrase regarding the first of these gifts: "prophecy, *in proportion to faith.*" (We will return to that, shortly.) And in naming the last three, he does not simply say they are *exercising* their gifts; he says *how* they are to exercise them. Had he been consistent in all three of these points, the list would have looked like this:

- The prophet, in prophesying

- The minister, in ministering

- The teacher, in teaching

- The exhorter, in exhorting

- The giver, in giving

- The leader, in leading

- The compassionate, in showing compassion

Once again, there are gifts on this list we have considered previously: prophecy, teaching, and leading. There are four gifts that were not on any of the lists we have already looked at: ministry, exhortation, giving, and being compassionate.

The qualifications Paul mentions with regard to *how* we are to prophesy, give, lead, and be compassionate give us clues as to how we might learn to use these gifts, as well.

Wright says:

> With most of the gifts in the list, the thrust of the commands is obvious: servers should serve, teachers should teach, and so on, with as much energy and skill as they can. This is clear with the second, third, and fourth "gifts," ministry (or "serving," NIV), teaching, and exhortation, where the word describing how one should exercise one's gift is simply the cognate word of the gift itself. The final three (giving, leading, showing compassion)

develop the idea slightly (givers should be generous, leaders should be diligent, compassion should be shown cheerfully), and this leads naturally into the more general commands of vv. 9–13.[127]

The giver is not just to give, but to give *generously*.

But are we not *all* to be givers? Indeed, in the very next paragraph he says (to all of us), "Contribute to the needs of the saints" (Rom. 12:13). But within the body of Christ, there are some who are called to a special ministry of giving far beyond what everyone else gives.

It might seem obvious that in order to do that, one would have to be wealthy. But remember the widow with her two tiny half-pennies: "Truly I tell you, this poor widow has put in more than all those who are contributing to the treasury. For all of them have contributed out of their abundance; but she out of her poverty has put in everything she had, all she had to live on" (Mark 12:43–44).

Some clergy, at stewardship time, tell their congregations to "give until it hurts." And some say, "Give until it stops hurting." In my congregation in Virginia, there was a man who lived for many years on what he called a "reverse tithe": he gave away 90 percent of what he earned and lived on the remaining 10 percent. Everyone in the congregation recognized him as having a special charism for giving, and for more than three decades he has led an organization called Christian Stewardship Ministries.

Those who want to know whether God has anointed them with that charism might try giving generously and see whether or not it stops hurting!

The leader is not simply to lead, but he or she is to be *diligent* in doing so.

Anyone can be assigned to do a task and organize others to help. But if that person is diligent in tackling the job, other assignments will follow, and quickly others in the congregation will recognize that the person in question has a charism for leadership.

All Christians are called to be compassionate, to the point of loving

---

127 Wright, "Romans," 711.

our enemies (Matt. 5:44). But there are those whose special joy comes from blessing the unlovely, the very difficult, and the desperately needy. One thinks of Father Damien among the lepers of Kalawo, Molokai.

The pattern here is very simple. We are to give ourselves to various ministries, and when we find ourselves doing those particular things especially well and finding great joy in them, we may begin to recognize that God has called us to "major" in those ministries and that he has given us a special anointing, a special charism, to do so. Others will probably recognize it as well.

Father Terry Fullam was internationally recognized as one of the great Bible teachers of the twentieth century. On many occasions he was heard to say, "I would rather spend six hours teaching than twenty minutes counseling." He found his charism (and he knew he did not have one for counseling!), and everyone recognized it with him.

There are those who have a special ministry within the body of Christ of exhortation: encouraging others to be and do all that God wants of them (Rom. 12:8).

And in this list, Paul uses for the first time the word "ministry" as one of the gifts of the Spirit. As we have seen throughout this study, and as we see in everyday life, "ministry" can be almost anything that we offer to God and to the members of Christ's body, and, indeed, to those who do not yet believe.

This leaves us with "prophecy, *in proportion to faith*." The most common interpretation of this phrase is that prophecy should be measured according to how well it builds up faith in those who hear it.[128] I want to suggest a very different interpretation.

Recall, again, that Paul told the Corinthians to "strive for the spiritual gifts, and especially that you may prophesy" (1 Cor. 14:1). He then said, "You can all prophesy one by one, so that all may learn and all be encouraged" (1 Cor. 14:31).

How does one learn to prophesy? First, by asking God for that gift

---

128   See, for instance, Brendon Byrne, "Romans," in *Sacra Pagina*, vol. 6 (Collegeville: Liturgical Press, 1996), 372.

(remembering that he distributes gifts "as the Spirit chooses" [1 Cor. 12:11]). *And then by trying to do it!*

Probably every one of us has had the experience, perhaps many times, of speaking with someone, or being in a group, and having a very strong urge to offer a word of encouragement, or perhaps correction or even rebuke. We have even wondered, *Is this something from God or is it just my own gut reaction?*

If it is one-on-one, it may be a prompting from the Holy Spirit to give an *exhortation*, a message intended to incite and encourage. If it is in a group, it may be a prompting to give a word of *prophecy*.

But in either case, what if we are wrong? We do not want to be wrong and in the process offend others. So we may well "bite our tongues." Hesitation to speak may "quench" the Spirit's desires in that instance (1 Thess. 5:19).

If we were absolutely convinced we had a message from God, we might be able to say with the prophets of old, "Thus says the Lord." But if the conviction is nowhere that strong, I suggest we might express it more tentatively: "I have the sense that the Lord might want us to consider (whatever it is). Does anyone confirm that?"

Paul says, "Let two or three prophets speak, and *let the others weigh what is said*" (1 Cor. 14:29).

If, indeed, the message is confirmed, we might be a bit more confident the next time this happens. And our confidence will continue to grow if God is, indeed, giving us this gift as a ministry. Our prophecies will grow stronger as we grow in the faith that they are really from God. We will learn to distinguish much more accurately when it *is* from him and not just something of our own.

We will prophesy in proportion to our faith that we are speaking from God.

In short, the teacher will learn to teach by teaching. The exhorter will learn to exhort by exhorting. The giver will learn to be a giver of great generosity by giving generously. The leader will learn to be a leader by being diligent in leading. The person with a special charism for compassion will learn compassion by finding joy in it. And the prophet will learn to be a prophet by prophesying in proportion to faith.

Those who give words of wisdom and knowledge will learn to do so by doing so. The healer and miracle worker will know they have those gifts because when they try to minister in those ways, God uses them.

The gifts of God are there for the blessing of his church. We need to ask for them, "try them out," and see which are ours.

A Lesson in "Ministry"

Bob came to see me one day. He said, "I work for the government in DC, and I am eligible for early retirement. I would like to take that and spend the rest of my life in ministry." I said, "Great. Why don't you take some of the courses we offer and see where God is leading you?"

We had courses in all kinds of ministry: personal evangelism, visiting the hospitalized and shut-in, leading Bible studies and prayer groups, working with children and young people, caring for the homeless, doing short-term mission trips, and so on.

Bob came to see me several months later. There were tears in his eyes as he said, "I have taken every course this church offers, and none of them are my ministry."

I said, "Bob, what do you like to do?"

He looked at me very strangely and said, "I don't want to brag, but I can do anything with my hands." "What do you mean?" "I can do carpentry, electricity, plumbing, brick-laying, wood working—just about anything; I just wish there were a ministry there."

I said, "Bob, the physical plant is yours."

We had a very large campus with a good deal of deferred maintenance. Bob started in one room, went on to the next, and then the next. It took a couple of years, but he personally, single-handedly renovated the whole plant: church, chapel, office building, education building, rectory.

Whenever anyone came into a room where Bob was working, it was like there was a little motor humming; he absolutely exuded the joy of the Lord.

By the time he was finished, he had a second career working in parishioners' homes, repairing and renovating as needed. If they could pay him, he accepted gratefully. If not, it was his gift to them.

"We have gifts that differ according to the grace given to us...ministry in ministering."

CHAPTER 22

THE FIVE CALLINGS

"Each of us was given grace according to the measure of
Christ's gift.... The gifts he gave were that some would be
apostles, some prophets, some evangelists, some pastors and
teachers, to equip the saints for the work of ministry, for
building up the body of Christ, until all of us come to the
unity of the faith and of the knowledge of the Son of God,
to maturity, to the measure of the full stature of Christ."

—EPHESIANS 4:7, 11–16

A LTHOUGH MANY TODAY believe the letter to the Ephesians was not actually written by St. Paul, we believe the case for the traditional view can still be made responsibly.[129] In any event, the letter carries forward Paul's discussion of the gifts of the Holy Spirit, using here the category *dorea* rather than the more familiar *charisma* or *charismata*. As noted previously, *dorea* may mean precisely an "office" rather than a "manifestation," *charisma*, though for the most part the words are used interchangeably.

The author discusses "the gifts Christ gave to his church" and mentions five of them in particular: apostles, prophets, evangelists, pastors, and teachers.

David Sheppard, the Bishop of Liverpool from 1975 to 1997, referred

---

129 Cf. Markus Barth, *Ephesians*, 2 vols. (Garden City: Doubleday, 1974); Peter T. O'Brien, *Letter to the Ephesians* (Grand Rapids: Eerdmans, 1999).

to these as "the five callings." These are *leadership callings,* all of which are crucial to the building up ("edification") of Christ's church.

(Some have argued that "pastors and teachers" are two ways of referring to the same persons; certainly most pastors are also—sometimes primarily—teachers. But some are not. Some members of the body who are deeply gifted as pastors are not at all gifted as teachers, and some teachers are not gifted as pastors. So we will agree with Bishop Sheppard that these are five, not four, callings.)

Clearly, in this passage, we have moved from *manifestations* of the Holy Spirit to ongoing and recognized *ministries* of the Holy Spirit, and now to *offices* in the church.

The two new categories are *evangelists* and *pastors.* Evangelists are the "baby doctors" of the ministry, those who proclaim the gospel in such ways that their hearers will come to an initial commitment to Christ. Evangelists move on after that happens.[130]

Billy Graham has proclaimed the gospel in person to far more people than has any other preacher in the history of the church. Throughout his lengthy career, he stayed in a given city only for the duration of his crusade. When he left, he encouraged the new converts to go to their local churches where the pastors would take over their nurture.

Pastors are there for the long haul, discipling the new converts and doing all they can to help them grow into maturity.[131]

It is worth pausing here to reflect on the need for shared or "mutual" ministry. A congregation could conceivably call as its pastor someone whose gifting from the Holy Spirit is either evangelism or pastoring. But (in spite of the fact that Paul was evidently both an evangelist and a pastor!) it is infrequently the case that one person will be strongly gifted in both areas. The "baby doctor" moves on, while the discipler stays for the long haul.

The "five callings" are ministry gifts we look for in those aspiring to be ordained. They are not *limited* to the ordained, but we hope that

---

130   Cf., Acts 16:30–31
131   Cf., Acts 20:20

those aspiring to be ordained by the church will be gifted in one or more of these areas of leadership.

The King James or Authorized Version of the Bible punctuated the sentence in a way that made it sound as if the purpose of these leadership gifts in the church was three-fold: "For the perfecting of the saints, for the work of the ministry, [and] for the edifying of the body of Christ."

But the first comma is very misleading. It makes it sound as if the work of the "minister" is to minister, and the work of the congregation is to congregate!

Paul is actually saying something very different. The job of the "minister" is "to equip the saints for the work of ministry," with the result being that the body of Christ will be built up and the further result that we will "come to the unity of the faith and of the knowledge of the Son of God, to maturity, to the measure of the full stature of Christ."

God wants his church to become everything his Son was and is!

But the "catch" is that we will get there *together*, or not at all. And we will get there together as the gifts of the Holy Spirit are dispensed among us, developed properly, and put to use in the context of love.

All the members of the body of Christ need to discover what their gifts are (more on that in the next chapter), develop them to their maximum capacity, and offer them to God and his church. The leaders in the church, especially the pastors, need to help the other members determine what their gifts are and deploy them for ministry. Careful supervision and accountability are required, as are correction and discipline, on occasion.

The author of Ephesians says:

> Speaking the truth in love, we must grow up in every way into him who is the head, into Christ, from whom the whole body, joined and knit together by every ligament with which it is equipped, as each part is working properly, promotes the body's growth in building itself up in love.
>
> —Ephesians 4:15–16

There are no "spare parts" in the body of Christ!

CHAPTER 23

As Good Stewards

"Serve one another with whatever gift each of you has received."

—1 Peter 4:10

THE FINAL LIST is not from Paul but from Peter, and it contains only two gifts. And they are both general rather than specific: "Whoever speaks must do so as one speaking the very words of God; whoever serves must do so with the strength that God supplies, so that God may be glorified in all things through Jesus Christ" (1 Pet. 4:11).

Speaking and serving—we have seen a wide variety of ways of doing both things. Peter now says that *whoever* does them must do so with the consciousness that God inspires the speaking and God supplies the strength for the serving.

We are nearly at the end of our survey.

There are a number of other "stand-alone" references to gifts of the Holy Spirit. Other *charisma* verses include 2 Corinthians 8:4 ("ministry to the saints"), Romans 6:23 ("eternal life"), 1 Corinthians 7:7–8 ("marriage and singleness"—and if you doubt you have a gift from God, hang on to this one! You are either married or single, and both states are called *charisms* of the Holy Spirit!), and 2 Corinthians 1:11 ("answered prayer").

Other *dorea* verses include John 4:10 ("living water"), Acts 2:38, 8:10, and 11:17 ("the Holy Spirit"), Hebrews 6:4 ("the Holy Spirit" concerning salvation), Romans 5:15 ("grace"), Romans 5:17 ("righteousness"), and 2 Corinthians 9:15, Ephesians 3:7, and 4:7 ("grace").

Some of the gifts of the Spirit are dramatically supernatural. Others are far less so. Some are behind the scenes but equally necessary for the body of Christ to do and be all God desires: "The members of the body that seem to be weaker are indispensable, and those members of the body that we think less honorable we clothe with greater honor, and our less respectable members are treated with greater respect" (1 Cor. 12:22–23).

If you were to ask me to help you identify the gifts you already have, I would ask you the following questions:

- *What do you like to do?* (cf. Bob, above.) If you *like* to do it, you are probably good at it. That may not always be the case. (Certainly there are those who should confine their singing to the shower!) But broadly speaking, if you enjoy doing something, it is probably because God has gifted you in that area, and offering that gift back to him and to his church is one of the keys to discovering your ministry.

- *What does God bless when you do it?* When you can observe good results from things you are personally responsible for, you may begin to conclude that God is anointing you for those good things. When you do (whatever), are people blessed by it? Are they drawn closer to the Lord? Do they have greater understanding of his purposes in their lives?

- *What does the body of Christ confirm?* When people tell you, "When you do *that* God blesses me," you know a gift of the Holy Spirit is likely to be in operation.

- *What need can you meet?* The Lord *never* allows us to see a problem so that we may become critics of it. He allows us to see a problem so we can become part of the solution for it. I used to love it when parishioners would come by and say things like, "We have to do something about the youth program!" I would reply, "Thank God you are going to do something about the youth program!"

A LESSON IN DEPLOYING MINISTRY

When I first began parish ministry, I thought of myself as a kind of "jack of all trades" spiritually. I genuinely enjoyed nearly every aspect of my responsibilities. I enjoyed preaching and teaching. I enjoyed counseling. I enjoyed meeting people in their homes, doing hospital visitations, and even (most) vestry meetings.

But I began to hear people say something that stood out: "When you teach, God blesses me." I finally realized God was trying to tell me something. If God *blesses* my teaching then I need to "major" in teaching. That means there have to be times when I teach and times for doing adequate preparation for teaching. And *that* means that some of the usual expectations people have regarding clergy (including my own expectations) need to be re-examined.

If I am going to give myself to a ministry that includes extensive teaching, perhaps routine hospital visitation, for instance, can become a lay ministry.

Fairfax, Virginia, is just outside the "beltway" that circles the District of Columbia. And we had parishioners coming from Virginia, Maryland, and the District. Often we had parishioners in various hospitals all the way around the beltway.

I could have spent all day, every day doing nothing but hospital visitation! And that would have been a good ministry. But if I was to give myself to teaching, hospital visitation could not be *my* ministry. If someone were in a very critical condition or facing the possibility of death, of course I would be there. But for most brief hospital visits, I thought this was a ministry I could train others to do.

So I invited anyone who wished to learn about doing hospital visitations to come take a brief course on the subject. It was pretty basic. I simply shared what I had learned about it by *doing it*. (Do not stay very long. Do not sit on the bed. Do ask if the patient wants to pray. Almost always the answer will be yes, but if it is not, pray for the person after you leave. Do *not* say, "You think that's bad? Let me tell you what happened to me!")

I suggested that the members of the class take one lunchtime during the coming week and visit the hospital nearest where they worked, check at the desk for Episcopalians in general, and members of our parish in particular, and then pay as many of them as possible a brief call.

When we reconvened the following week, some of the members said (like Bob), "That is *not* my ministry!" But others asked, "Can we do this more than once a week?" (They were showing compassion with cheerfulness!)

They experienced the joy of discovering God could use them in this particular ministry, and they wanted more of it. And I exercised my gift to multiply myself and provide far more hospital ministry than I could have done by myself.

God gives his gifts so his people, the members of the body of his Son, may be equipped to do whatever is necessary to meet the needs of the needy. It is our responsibility as members of the body to discover what our gifts are, develop them to the fullest extent possible, ask him for additional gifts for ministry as he sees fit, and deploy whatever he gives in the service of his church.

CHAPTER 24

OUR COMMISSION

"Obey everything I have commanded you."
—MATTHEW 28:20

IN THIS STUDY, we have explored the ministry of Jesus as an expression of the anointing and the gifts of the Holy Spirit. We looked in detail at the more dramatic and controversial gifts that St. Paul lists in the first half of 1 Corinthians 12, and we saw that all of those gifts—with the possible exception of tongues and interpretation—were abundantly evident in Jesus's life and ministry.

Our best illustrations of what the gifts are and how they work is found in Jesus himself. He exercised a ministry of "signs and wonders," and he "called the twelve together and gave them power and authority over all demons and to cure diseases, and he sent them out to proclaim the kingdom of God and to heal" (Luke 9:1–2). Later, he appointed seventy others to do the same.[132]

We moved on to a second list at the end of 1 Corinthians 12, and we noticed that the distinction so often made between supernatural gifts and natural talents is not present in the New Testament. We saw that *all* of the gifts of the Holy Spirit, whether dramatic and up front or much more behind the scenes are given so we can better serve the Lord and each other, and they are *all* "activated by one and the same

---

132   Luke 10:1ff. Some of the texts read seventy-two.

Spirit, who allots to each one individually just as the Spirit chooses" (1 Cor. 12:11).

Some of the gifts are manifestations of the Holy Spirit that appear occasionally. Some are ministries that are developed through repeated use. Some are offices recognized by the church. And some simply involve God giving us the ability to live into his calling, whatever it might be.

We looked at "the love chapter," in 1 Corinthians 13, a kind of interruption in Paul's extended discussion of the gifts of the Spirit. We were reminded that unless the gifts are exercised within the context of love, we will have completely missed the point.

We saw that sometimes God gives gifts that enable his people to endure demanding callings, up to and including extreme poverty and even martyrdom.

We noted that Paul urged us three times in a row to strive for the gifts of the Holy Spirit. They were essential for Jesus's ministry, for that of the twelve and the seventy, and they are essential for our ministries, whatever they may be. We considered what striving for the gifts might mean and concluded it involves earnestly desiring them and *asking* God to give them according to his good pleasure.

We then moved on to the other lists of gifts in Romans 12, Ephesians 4, and 1 Peter 4, and noted a number of stand-alone gifts that, in all (in the NRSV), total thirty-two different words or phrases naming gifts, some being at least partly synonymous with others. Nowhere is there an exhaustive list of gifts, but they are all God's equipment, empowerment, or enabling for us to do the things he is calling us to do and to meet the needs of others. We saw that the key to the work of the Holy Spirit in the church of Jesus Christ is: *all the fruit for all the Christians, and different gifts for different Christians.*

Peter said, "Each [and every one of you] has received a gift" (1 Pet. 4:10, RSV). And Paul named even marriage and singleness as charisms of the Holy Spirit (1 Cor. 7:7–8). So, let us stop dividing up the body of Christ into those who *have* and those who *have not* been gifted by the Holy Spirit! Each and every one of us has already received at least one gift, and Scripture encourages us to strive for additional gifts, especially those that will be of the greatest blessing to Christ's church.

Perhaps it is appropriate to conclude where we began. The last words that Matthew records Jesus speaking to his disciples were what we have come to call the Great Commission:

> All authority in heaven and on earth has been given to me. Go *therefore* and make disciples of all nations, baptizing them in the name of the Father and of the Son and of the Holy Spirit, and *teaching them to obey everything that I have commanded you.* And remember, I am with you always, to the end of the age.
>
> —MATTHEW 28:18–20

He said, "All authority has been given unto *me,* therefore *you* go." The "therefore" functions in only one way: *"you* are to go in *my* authority." He is sharing it with us.

We are to proclaim the gospel, make disciples, baptize them, and teach them to obey *everything* Jesus taught his first followers. That surely includes ministry in the power of the Spirit. Jesus is the chief example. The Holy Spirit enables us as he enabled him, and his gifts are the equipment for ministry.

For Further Reading

Attlee, Rosemary. *Renewal*. October/November. 1984.

Barclay, William. *The Gospel of John*. Vol. 1. Revised edition. Louisville: Westminster, 1975.

Barth, Karl. *Church Dogmatics*. Vol. 4. Edinburgh: T and T Clark, 1958.

Barth, Markus. *Ephesians*. Vols. 1 and 2. Garden City: Doubleday, 1974.

Bennett, Dennis and Rita. *The Holy Spirit and You*. Plainfield: Logos International, 1971.

Bilezikian, Gilbert. *Beyond Sex Roles*. Grand Rapids: Baker, 1985.

Boring, M. Eugene. "The Gospel of Matthew." In *The New Interpreter's Bible*. Vol. 8. Nashville: Abingdon, 1995.

Bruner, Frederick Dale. *A Theology of the Holy Spirit*. Grand Rapids: Eerdmans, 1970.

Bruner, Frederick Dale and William Hordern. *The Holy Spirit: Shy Member of the Trinity*. Minneapolis: Augsburg Publishing House, 1984.

Buttrick, George A. *The Interpreter's Bible*. Vol. 7. New York: Abingdon Press, 1951.

Byrne, Brendon. "Romans." In *Sacra Pagina*. Vol. 6. Collegeville: Liturgical Press, 1996.

Christenson, Larry, ed. *Welcome, Holy Spirit: A Study of Charismatic Renewal in the Church*. Minneapolis: Augsburg Publishing House, 1987.

Collins, Raymond F. "First Corinthians." In *Sacra Pagina*. Vol. 7. Collegeville: Liturgical Press, 1999.

Cowman, L. B. *Streams in the Desert*. Grand Rapids: Zondervan, 1997.

Donahue, John R. and Daniel J. Harrington. "The Gospel of Mark." In *Sacra Pagina*. Vol. 2. Collegeville: Liturgical Press, 2002.

Dunn, James D. G. "According to the Spirit of Jesus." *Theological Renewal* 5 (February–March 1997).

Dockery, D. S. "Baptism." In *Dictionary of Jesus and the Gospels*. Downers Grove: InterVarsity Press, 1992.

Ferguson, Sinclair B. *The Holy Spirit*. Downers Grove: InterVarsity Press, 1996.

Flokstra Jr., Gerard J. *The New Testament Study Bible*. Vol. 2. Springfield: Complete Biblical Library, 1988.

Frodsham, Stanley Howard. *Smith Wigglesworth: Apostle of Faith*. Springfield: Gospel Publishing House, 1972.

Grudem, Wayne. *Systematic Theology*. Grand Rapids: Zondervan, 1994.

Harrington, Daniel J. "The Gospel of Matthew." In *Sacra Pagina*. Vol. 1. Collegeville: Liturgical Press, 2007.

Holy Men, Holy Women. New York: Church Publishing, 2010.

Howe, John W. and Sam C. Pascoe. *Our Anglican Heritage*. Second edition. Eugene: Wipf and Stock, 2010.

Hummel, Charles E. *Fire in the Fireplace: Contemporary Charismatic Renewal*. Downers Grove: InterVarsity Press, 1978.

Kuyper, Abraham. *The Work of the Holy Spirit*. Trans. H. De Vries. New York: Funk and Wagnalls, 1900.

Lampe, G. W. H. *God as Spirit*. Oxford: Clarendon Press, 1977.

Lewis, C. S. *Mere Christianity*. New York: Macmillan, 1972.

———. *Miracles: A Preliminary Study*. New York: Macmillan, 1947.

Mallone, George. *Those Controversial Gifts*. Downers Grove: InterVarsity Press, 1983.

Napier, B. D. "Prophet, Prophetism." In *The Interpreter's Dictionary of the Bible*. Nashville: Abingdon Press, 1962.

O'Brien, Peter T. *Letter to the Ephesians*. Grand Rapids: Eerdmans, 1999.

O'Day, Gail R. "Commentary on John." In *The New Interpreter's Bible*. Vol. 9. Nashville: Abingdon Press, 1995.

Pinnock, Clark H. *Flame of Love: A Theology of the Holy Spirit*. Downers Grove: Inter Varsity Press, 1996.

Pytches, David. *Come, Holy Spirit*. London: Hodder and Stoughton, 1985.

Samply, J. Paul. "First Corinthians." In *The New Interpreter's Bible*. Vol. 10. Nashville: Abingdon Press, 2002.

Spencer, F. Scott. "Exorcism." In *The New Interpreter's Dictionary of the Bible*. Vol. 2. Nashville: Abingdon, 2007.

Strier, Richard. "Martin Luther and the Real Presence in Nature." *Journal of Medieval and Early Modern Studies* 37 (2007): 271–303.

Thomas, W. H. G. *The Holy Spirit of God*. Grand Rapids: Eerdman's, 1963.

Tuttle, Robert G. *The Partakers*. Nashville: Abingdon Press, 1974.

Wagner, C. Peter. *Your Spiritual Gifts*. Ventura: Regal, 2005.

Whitacre, Rodney A. *John*. In *The IVP New Testament Commentary Series*. Downers Grove: InterVarsity Press, 1999.

Williams, Charles B. *The New Testament: A Private Translation in the Language of the People*. Chicago: Moody Press, 1960.

Wright, N. T. "Romans." In *The New Interpreter's Bible*. Vol. 10. Nashville: Abingdon Press, 1992.